What people are saying about

Are You a Mutant?

You will recognize yourself in this book. Raquel's wisdom flows from each page. You will discover why it hasn't worked out for you yet & what to do to watch your life become magical – in a humorous, light way. Raquel has a way of explaining the unexplainable. Her personal story is funny, touching & enchanting, and it illustrates the work perfectly. I highly recommend the book as a means of stepping into who you were meant to be and manifesting all that you want.

Kathryn Alice, best-selling author of *Love Will Find You*

T0270419

Also by This Author
Thoth Book of Magic: A Daily Guide To Manifest The Life Your Soul Intended: A Sacred Toolbox with Step by Step Guidance To Awaken Your Divine Purpose, Power & Path
Publisher: BlissLife Press; 2nd edition (March 25, 2016)
ISBN: 9780997739237

Are You a Mutant?

Step by Step Human Design Guide to Unleash Your Genius, Understand your Uniqueness, and Thrive During Times of Transformation

Are You a Mutant?

Step by Step Human Design Guide to
Unleash Your Genius, Understand your
Uniqueness, and Thrive During
Times of Transformation

Raquel Reyna

Winchester, UK
Washington, USA

JOHN HUNT PUBLISHING

First published by O-Books, 2023
O-Books is an imprint of John Hunt Publishing Ltd., 3 East St., Alresford,
Hampshire SO24 9EE, UK
office@jhpbooks.com
www.johnhuntpublishing.com
www.o-books.com

For distributor details and how to order please visit the 'Ordering' section on our website.

ISBN: 978 1 80341 112 5
978 1 80341 113 2 (ebook)
Library of Congress Control Number: 2021951511

A CIP catalogue record for this book is available from the British Library.

Book Cover Credit to Davidian Lyon
Design: Matthew Greenfield

UK: Printed and bound by CPI Group (UK) Ltd, Croydon, CR0 4YY
Printed in North America by CPI GPS partners

We operate a distinctive and ethical publishing philosophy in
all areas of our business, from our global network of authors to
production and worldwide distribution.

Contents

Dedication

Dedicated to my beloved, Davidian Lyon, to whom I am forever grateful for not only mutating my path entirely, but for courageously living your Design side by side with me. And, of course, Ra Uru Hu, patient zero, the original mutant.

Foreword

Written by Kathryn Alice, a bestselling author with an internationally known brand. She is one of the most successful life coaches in the world. Kathryn has been featured in *Psychology Today*, *Parade* magazine, *The New York Times*, AP, *Daily Mail*, *Body and Soul* magazine, on *Montel* and NBC. She was featured as an expert in the feature film *Secrets of Love*.

I first met Raquel when she attended one of my workshops. At that time, she was looking for her path. As I blossomed into a bestselling author with a large following, I watched Raquel blossom, too. I supported her in meeting her soulmate and perfect business partner, as well as leaving her corporate career and believing she could get the book published. As someone who has traveled this path, it was clear that Raquel was also a natural-born author, a voice to be heard and able to manifest in her own life in her own way, as well.

Raquel's journey is inspiring. It wasn't until she discovered what you will learn in this book that she grew into the powerhouse teacher, leader and author she is today.

Are You a Mutant? is the key that many have been looking for. If you have felt out of place, have been frustrated with life not giving you what you wanted, or have felt misunderstood, this process will show you why that is and how to change it. No longer will you try to fit in where you don't. No longer will you be unfulfilled, angry, or misunderstood.

I had never heard of the Human Design System before Raquel introduced me to it. And it makes so much sense! It's a pointer toward that inner voice that leads you exactly where you want to go. It's a change mechanism with rich tools to apply it for concrete manifestation. Raquel breaks it down into simple, easy-to-apply steps that anyone can do. Her explanation shows clearly why most people are living lives they don't want, feeling unfulfilled, frustrated and helpless. Or feeling stressed out and angry. But further, it shows you how to quit being stuck.

It's hard not to race through the material. Each sentence is a giant AHA – enlightening, ringing so true that you want to shout, "Yes! That's IT!!!" Not only will you begin to understand yourself better, but you'll see others differently, know a better way of interacting with them, and understand their own motivation and way of being that is different than your own. You'll know what makes you and others tick.

As much as you find yourself wanting to race through the book, leaping from revelation to revelation, it is to be savored. Raquel packs a great deal of valuable wisdom and insight into every sentence. It's best to read a bit and then digest it, putting what you learn into practice. Her examples make the work come alive. And break it down into a practical application that will change everything for you.

In the end, you'll come away from the book with a Personal Success Code unique to you. You can use this code and your new understanding of this system to immediately feel at peace and joyful, armed with a new guidance, a sure-footed way into the life of your dreams. Off you will go, making changes with ease, no longer struggling or falling short.

This book will align you with who you really are. Just by being exposed to this material, you will be changed. It is impossible not to thrive with the new awareness that *Are You a Mutant?* fosters.

I'm honored to present this book to you. And I'm blessing you for this being your ticket into the life you've always wanted – a life of happiness, fulfillment, love & joy at every turn. *Are You a Mutant?* and Raquel will take you there.

Acknowledgements

This book encompasses a lifetime of discovery and experiential learning; there are many people to thank who have conspired with me along the way. So many unique beings have supported me in bringing this book to fruition, inspiring, encouraging, and giving me wisdom and hope. This book would not exist with the life contributions of so many people, including:

My publishing team at John Hunt Publishers and O-Books who have believed in this vision and given it a platform.

My family, particularly my sister Marilee and brother Jeff, whose brilliance luckily rubbed off on me after hours and hours of at-home tutoring sessions. The incalculable support I received from my treasured inner circle BFFs of both my queens and goddesses; you all know who you are, and I am forever grateful for you. All of my teachers, particularly Michael David Gilardy, my spiritual father, who took me in when I needed spiritual insight and guidance, let me sleep on the couch for a year decompressing from life, and taught me so much of what I know energetically. My clients who have been studying with me over the last couple of years: their dedication and incredible commitment to this wisdom, and their own personal experimentation with this work created the most juicy, satisfying, thriving community of successful visionaries that I am grateful for every day. I particularly want to thank my Creative Coaching Certification students, Four Radical Transformations, and Rave Cosmology groups that transformed the way I taught and brought forward this knowledge because of their co-creation power. Davidian, my beloved life and business partner to whom this book is dedicated. Anne Saint Francis Hughes, wherever you are, thanks for changing my life. A special thanks to Kathryn Alice, who believed in my vision and fortified me with insights on manifesting my beloved partner, knowing I could successfully become a published author, as well as manifesting my popular online company. And of course, thank you to my Mom and Dad who both earned their wings and use them every day to help guide my life.

Chapter 1

How Are You Designed to Live?

If one is not a sage or a Saint, the best we can do, in the field of metaphysics, is to study the works of those who were, and who, because they had modified their merely human mode of being, were capable of a more than merely human kind and amount of knowledge.
Aldous Huxley

The intention of this book is to bring forward a complex body of information that often takes on a very intellectual form, and because of this, its value often goes unnoticed. The body of knowledge is a system of change. A profound body of knowledge that will assist you in getting to know yourself and others in your life in a reflective and new life-affirming way. Imagine if I said, I am about to give you a decoder of your DNA genetic blueprint: it reveals who you are, your life purpose, the best strategy to live a successful life, and how to make decisions to lead you towards the life you were designed for. Would you think that was too good to be true? I did too at first, and yes, of course, there is a caveat. Most of you are so conditioned out of the truth of who you are that even if I give you the entire code to deciphering your individual unique reason for existence, there will still be a lot of work unlearning all the things society, your parents, your schooling, all told you to be. So, there is that. Also, once you realize you have been living as your NOT-SELF, or as you were conditioned, you might be so alarmed that you scream heresy and simply run the other direction. In essence, the material is a personal gold mine to excavate your soul, but like anything, you must be willing and available for this possibility. So, it is for those courageous enough to discover the truth. A sort of red pill/blue pill question. If you are part of the courageous ones who want to know the truth, then you are in the right place. The journey is deep, powerful, and explosive but also courageous.

So, if you are ready, let's jump down the rabbit hole together. If I only have a few of you, then so be it. It doesn't take many to shift the planet. So take my hand and let's jump in together. It is scary but exhilarating. Yes, you will never be the same, and once you realize this, you will be so excited to live as your authentic new, unshackled self!

The system I am going to break down for you is called Human Design. But beware: I am a heretic here to shock your initiation into this system, convince you it is worth doing, and ignite the material in a forward-thinking, spiritually progressive new way. The beauty of this work is that I will be introducing you to the art of differentiation. Meaning we are not all here to see the world alike. It is not to be debated or argued by the intellectual dark web. Because even though you might be able to see both sides to the argument, this work transcends the limitation of the intellect as the one true God. It purports there is a pearl of greater wisdom than the mind if you dare to let go of your homage to the intellect. There is nothing to debate here, no reason to disagree. You can try this on, and if it works for you, you might just find yourself living a more fulfilled life, period. This presentation may not appeal to all, particularly if you are already adhering to a specific body of Human Design intel that says it should only be taught one way. So no worries. If this is not your cup of tea, follow your own IA and find the teachings that resonate with your fractal. However, if you are curious and have heard of this system before, my intention is that you will be reintroduced to it in a new way, and if this is new for you, hold on, it is a wild ride.

So, I am a Personal View. (Whenever I use terms specifically from the system of Human Design, I will capitalize the terms.

If you don't immediately understand the term, you will by the end of the book. Or I will list the term and definition in the accompanying PDF you can get at: https://foxy5d.com/pages/are-you-a-mutant.)

This book is going to be part storytelling, part personal journey, and part educational classroom. Personal View means I see things through my lens and my own journey. I also believe we all learn by experience, not just knowledge. We can read and think all we want, but it is very surface until we try it on and begin to live it. So as I share this intel, I will also integrate my own story and encourage you not to believe what I am saying, BUT TRY IT ON in your life. If these strategies work for you, IE makes a noticeable change in your life after you give a thorough college try – not proverbial lip service. Then this material is for you! Living it might align you to a much more satisfying, successful, peace-driven, and awe-inspiring life. Please experiment with the strategies I will share with you (don't just think about them, don't just read them, don't just put them by the nightstand). Download them into action in your life. Then you might just emerge an entirely new expression of your unique genius.

Take a breath in with me here – it is TRUTH. (Not a Human Design word, but a concept of epistemology truth not to be compared to a true/false paradigm, an ever-present TRUTH.) What is truth, you ask? That you are unique. If you are like 100% (well OK 98%) of humanity, the uniqueness of who you are was beaten out of you so that you fit in, not purposefully, but this is how the collective operates. There is a whirlwind conditioning force that shoves everyone into a round hole, and let's just say some of the square pegs are even more uniquely shaped than a square. These unique angels and edges have been brutally shaved off (not permanently) so that the group, the clique, the company, the family accept you. Now is the time to see those parts of yourself and let your authentic distinctiveness

SHINE! Once you do, you will feel free, awake, on fire, blessed to be alive, excited to get up, relieved that you can finally let go of pretending, trying to be liked, or trying to fit in; all that will be over. You are finally given a free pass to live like yourself!

I am a seeker. I have always sought out and searched for the unknowable. I always asked the super hard questions like: why are we here, why am I alive, what is my purpose? These types of questions do not go unnoticed by the Universe. If you sincerely seek answers, you will eventually find them. So on my journey, I have come across many answers. Some were interesting, others were BS, a few were mind-boggling, and some literally gave me tools to live a more soul-fulfilling and successful life that actually worked. I am a mystic but also incredibly grounded and practical. So, I intend to bring you tools you can take home with you in bite-sized pieces that might cataclysmically transform your life if you also long for this, as I did.

Chapter 2

To Understand the End, You Must Start from the Beginning

The Law of Divine Compensation posits that this is a self-organizing and self-correcting universe. The embryo becomes a baby, the bud becomes a blossom, the acorn becomes an oak tree. Clearly, there is some invisible force that is moving every aspect of reality to its next best expression.
Marianne Williamson

To touch this vast complex topic and break it down into pocket-sized small pieces which you can take home into your life and feast on for the next couple days or weeks of reading this book, I need to give a little background. My background. As you begin to perceive your own Not-Self life, there begins an inevitable unraveling of realities you may have created for yourself. Who you thought you were stops recreating frustration with its actions, which can be disorienting at first. It is a fascinating moment when you come to this intel, what led you to it, what transpired before the swallowing of the RED PILL, and what happens after the seven-year transformation. Yes, they say it takes a full seven years to Decondition regardless of how much therapy or inner work you have already done on yourself. So, slow down; you can't rush this. Grab some tea, coffee, green juice, wine, your choice, and let's go on this journey together! Because I am in awe of this transformation in myself, it is so clear looking back on my past how my NOT-Self life ran the ship. As I point out my own insight of self, I hope that it will help you look back over your life and witness any Not-Self aspects that were in charge of your life choices.

As a seeker, I have always been a devoted student of wisdom.

Nothing created such massive revelatory shifts in me as diving into my Human Design chart, even after years of studying self-help, mysticism, shamanism, spiritual psychology, and oh so much more. At university, a world did open up to me, inspired by my innate connection to the unseen forces. I always knew I was connected to "imaginary little friends," lucid dreams, and parallel worlds. But these types of things were never discussed in the San Fernando Valley where I grew up. But in college, things changed; this stuff got real. It all started when I cracked open my first metaphysical book, and I immediately became a voracious reader. Talk about going from black and white to color, this *Wizard of Oz*-infused colorful world took on an unbelievably profound spiritual awakening in my psyche. The mysteriously magical doors of a world beyond the mundane began to open. Several books unleashed this new fervor within me, *Seth Speaks*, *Kryon*, *The Law of One*, the *I Ching*, and eventually, I found the Carlos Castaneda book series.

I read all eight books, one after the other of the Don Juan teachings. I read everywhere: at the pool, in class, walking down the street with pages pulled apart, marked in red, underlined, and nose buried inside. Why had no one even mentioned to me that this type of thing existed? I don't think I had ever heard of Shamanism. Where I grew up, there was Hollywood, getting ahead, living in the most prominent house on the block or in Brentwood, marrying well, being hot, being famous, and really not much else. Please forgive me; this is a horribly unfair statement to the LA I have come to love today. But where and when I grew up, there was no mention of metaphysics, spirituality, shamanism, mysticism, or anything that smelled of what some people might refer to today as, "woo." I never knew any of this existed. So, how is it that this entirely rich deep world of metaphysics, quantum science, intuitive medicine, fractal geometry, personal transformation, spiritual concepts existed, and not one person I knew even mentioned it? I was baffled. But here is a tip, don't run home and share the news about multiple universes, 12 dimensions, seeing people who have transitioned, or speaking with long-dead gurus. Let's just say it's uninvited.

After completing Carlos Castaneda's entire series, I went to bed with a powerful calling and intention that I voiced to no one in particular, "I want to meet my shamanic teacher."

It was a very loud and clear invocation.

The next day, a friend told me about a fellow student teaching The Four Agreements out of his living room. Now, mind you, this was before this was a best-selling *New York Times* book. Yes, it was don Miguel Ruiz's son teaching the knowledge from his college apartment living room.

They both came from the Toltec lineage, which was the same lineage as Carlos Castaneda.

When I walked into the empty living room with four college students sitting in a circle preparing to meditate, I was struck immediately with the power of this moment. Not only did this meeting change everything I ever believed to be true about the world and my reality. It also made me realize for the very first time my inner world, my thoughts, my intentions to the unseen Universe are f-ing being heard!

This invocation changed the entire trajectory of my life.

A true shaman has the power to shift the entire dimension you walk in. The introduction to the Dream of this world, and how we create our own reality were all introduced to me.

I took it very seriously. I went to every class Miguel, his son, or anyone from the community offered. I took every trip, every class, and did every dream Mitote event I could do. (A dream Mitote is an all-night energetic dreaming ceremony provided by the Toltec shamanic leader.) I basically got an additional PhD degree in metaphysics and shamanism while still finishing my BA degree.

When I graduated, I made a radical choice to follow my spiritual path rather than accept a full-paid scholarship to

NYU graduate school. This choice led me to a mysterious and beautifully mystical ecosphere. I leaped off a cliff with my teachers to travel all over the world and discover there is definitely more to the eye than what schools are teaching, including all of the universities. The shamans, enlightened teachers, gurus, mystics of the world know this, and now it is becoming a much more common study. Still, it is not mainstream. It was the ONLY way for me.

We traveled to Europe, Egypt, Israel, Peru, including Machu Picchu, Mexico, and the Teotihuacan Pyramids, and it was there I had a vision. It was multidimensional, colorful, with all forces pointing to the power within me to create this vision.

The multisensory vision took place on top of the Pyramid of the Sun. Teotihuacan is a sacred land which many Toltecs use now and have used in the past as a place of transformation. It is said to be the land where man learns to walk as God. I walked in light for days and awakened to a profound truth within me: the light was love. The love was truth, and the vision was one I needed to manifest.

I felt this love and purity so powerfully that it was a sacred source within me that nourished and led me all of my life. This love spoke to me, guided me, and, most importantly, picked me up during my lowest moments. And after this awakening, there definitely were some low moments to follow, as most people who have had spiritual openings can relate. It is the suffering if we let it, that can lead us to awaken even more deeply. For me, the spiritual introductions were followed by confusion, missteps, and lots of professional blunders, only to leave me spinning and seeking once again. It was a process, and why it is so important as a backdrop for the Human Design intel that I will be integrating into this book. Often another piece of knowledge brings more questioning, so I wanted to lay out the levels of investigation I have already been through to sew together the fabric of integrating Human Design into a life. It is a powerful tool to tie all the pieces together.

Where there may have been leaps into failed business ventures, spiritual awakenings that led to confusion, or journeys in self-help that led to disappointment, you will come to understand how you may have misperceived these teachings as I did. You may see through my mistakes how many spiritual teachings might just lead you to paths that are not correct for you, and this will perhaps allow you, my fellow journeyer, to sort through your past misperceptions and finally awaken a life that reflects your truth.

You see, after I had this vision, I decided I should go out and manifest this clear insight that was handed to me in such a magical way up there on that fateful night atop the Pyramid of the Sun. This desire to go out and make your vision come to life is a common misstep for many people on a spiritual path that can cause a lot of pain, frustration, bitterness if you are unaware of your Design.

It did for me big time. You see, I was very young and full of enthusiasm, so I headed to San Francisco to create the vision I saw on top of the pyramid. A 13-member performance band that I saw had the power to be like a Stomp/Blue Man Group type of experience that could bring spiritual transformation to the world. WOW, was I wrong in the most profound life-defeating way. It was, however, a fun and colorful journey that did lead to success. Within a few short years, we ran in a theater in downtown San Francisco five days a week for a 300-seat audience. We performed with some massive names like Jane's Addiction and War, and it was a hugely outwardly successful manifestation.

Now to wrap up my entire 20s in a paragraph is no small feat. There was so much drama. Just think tsunami, egos, drugs, narcissism, power games, and the fact that I was a Line 5 Projector who pushed the vision into existence. No one actually recognized me as the visionary of the group; everyone stole the work and the idea at every step. I have the Motivation of Innocence, and basically, I was living out 100% my Not-Self Transference theme of Desire. (This is an area of Human Design; some of you might know what I am referring to, and some do not. More on these topics will be in the accompanying PDF if I lost some of you.) I could dedicate an entire book to this experience, so I will keep it brief in this one.

Needless to say, I was not recognized as the leader. I was excruciatingly bitter, and the drama was so intense it ate me alive. In typical Line 5 fashion, I was violently pushed from the pedestal. (Don't worry, I will spare you the gory 20-year-old drama details.) And had to leave the entire city of San Francisco pronto.

Most Line 5s who have had entire groups of people project onto them might relate.

So, one day I packed up the Miata and drove down the coast to San Diego with about $300 in my pocket. My entire life in a two-seater convertible with no back seat. At that time, my career fell apart, and I was deeply confused about all spiritual messages. I had no idea what I wanted to do next. I had no fundamental skills other than manifesting a Stomp-like rock band (which doesn't translate to many other job positions). Lost, spinning and profoundly bewildered. At this stage of my life, I had still not been introduced to Human Design. OYE. It was what many people would now call a proverbial shit show.

Chapter 3

Living with Enlightened Teachers – Talk About a Chemical Change

An enlightened teacher has personal power. Sitting and meditating with an enlightened teacher in a meditation hall or at a power spot can change you forever. To encounter such a being is considered the ultimate karmic blessing in the sense that your life will be so configured that every single variant of problematic karma will surface, which means you have the opportunity of passing through them all correctly, going over the ocean of the samsara and reaching nirvana yourself.

Frederick Lenz

As I said I was clueless about being a Projector who was, of course, so exhausted from what happened in San Francisco that I ended up in San Diego crashing out on Michael's couch for a year. In typical Projector style. But this was no ordinary year. As life would unfold, I would say it was one of the most magical enchanted years of my existence. So, there is no other way to put this, except during this year along with Michael, I would be living with an extraordinary woman named Anne Francis. To be dramatic, she was an awakened master traveling the earth.

At this time, I wouldn't realize just how extraordinary this was. I was still young and had very little to compare the experience with. Now, as a mature adult who has been to Agape, received my Master's Degree in Spiritual Psychology, I have seen many spiritual teachers, all of whom were amazing. Still, nothing near what I saw with Anne Francis, and I would never see or hear of anything comparable again. Not on any YouTube channel, TV show, or news station. You see, the most authentic awakened masters are not those you see out there in the limelight. They are usually not being revered or famous. She would travel the world.

People searched for her wherever she was. She didn't charge for her work. The phone would ring nonstop when she was in town for people to beg for a chance to come and sit with her. You see, you couldn't pay your way to an appointment. She was either guided at the moment to see that person or not. If it was a no, it didn't matter how far you traveled to have a session with her; there was nothing you could do.

Her energy would shift those around her in mammoth ways. It took me decades to unpack that year.

She didn't live in this dimension; the world bent around her. I was mesmerized by her, all she did, her energy, her lifestyle. She would tell us, "I never know if I will ever see you again," every time she was called to another country. She came and left Michael's house without us knowing when or if she would return. Or how long she would be gone, or how she managed to buy tickets to travel the world at any given moment. Money, airline tickets, clothing, jewelry all just manifested in mysteriously mystical ways. Most of the time, people would just give her money because we knew she didn't charge for her work, or send her tickets to come and be with them. The flow was indeed one of the most miraculous things I have ever witnessed.

I think it's important to notice that once someone reaches a certain level of mastery or enlightenment, the world is entirely different. I witnessed this in mouth-dropping awe. However, I also realized no matter how many moments of enlightenment I felt in her presence or while traveling, I am not awakened. I am far from it, so I need tools and dedication. I need systems to understand myself on deeper levels and understand why I am here. Most people do, so please don't confuse the "woke" culture with true enlightenment. However, it's good to know true enlightenment is possible, but a very rare sighting. A teacher not sleeping with the students, seeking fame or fortune, an authentic master who has transcended this realm, is unbelievable but possible.

I would never be the same after this year. Michael, now David, is also an excellent spiritual teacher and leader who brought forward, and still to this day, brings forward many higher dimensional messages of divine light. His teachings have also changed many people on deep levels, and me. He was deemed one of the Naguals in the Miguel lineage but left the community to unleash his own mystical, galactic, shamanic teachings.

However, even with these spiritual experiences and awakenings, I could not understand how to live practically, make a living, or discover a meaningful career that embodied my truth. Of course, I knew of the Secret, the Law of Attraction, but these tools never appeared to work for me in the same way they did for others. This desire to have a career I loved nourished me, paid me well, and recognized my uniqueness always baffled me while simultaneously driving me to a more profound knowledge of myself.

When I did align with a company for my next career, it was an environment where I had to kind of stuff it down and go out and make some money so I could pay my bills. That sort of theme. Put that crazy multidimensional experience away, because I just could not make any sense of how Anne did what she did. So I wondered, how I could vibrate high enough to have life unfold more effortlessly? But it simply always eluded me. In other words, she was an incredible living example of what is possible, but she came without the "how to" manual. How to live spiritually, awaken, pay the bills, live in an enlightened 5D world, and still have a mortgage and pay off the credit cards. She did it seamlessly but never explained the how. So as you might imagine, this was incredibly altering and confusing for me.

It was a power journey. My life had always been one of adventure, freedom, then on to the next experience. Only many, I mean many, years later in the depth of my Human Design journey would any of this make sense to me. Quick HD recap of this portion of my life for those who know Human Design. I am a 25-51 on the Initiation through shock to discover my spiritual teacher. The Line 5 heresy pushed me out of San Francisco and into the shamanic initiation of awakening. The Gates of Madness and Undefined Head always put pressure on me to seek the unknowable. I would soon discover I am great at sales, 26-44, but all I could do was smell a rat at this point of the story. This means I did not trust any sales or allowing myself to buy into any type of "business of life coaching" that might support me on the material plane. It also allowed me to recognize when Anne lived on the planet and taught without charging for her work but walked on the earth with only a suitcase, watching the world unfold for her. I knew she was the real deal – a genuine, miraculous, life-altering, black swan sighting.

During this year, I stumbled into a boutique fitness center and was recognized immediately as someone who could serve women in health, fitness, and business. It turned out to be the fastest-growing franchise in the history of the US and began my next life journey.

This company recognized me for many years until I wasn't. It would support me in only working a few hours a day. I began to awaken the highest expression of this Channel of Surrender. It took me a couple of years to discover my Design and step into my Projector power (or even discover my Aura Type). However, these years with the corporate career – I can see why this worked for as long as it did, looking back from the bird's eye view of my Human Design knowledge. I was recognized; I could work from home with my own schedule; I was invited in by the owner of the original facility to manage her store after she learned about my dance and business background.

I was in my joy; it was a pure and straightforward system for a successful business. Invitations do not last forever. Eventually, if they are revoked, you can feel it. When your soul is ready to be completely realized, recognized, or more awakened to your next level, the invitations get rescinded. Situations that were once comfortable and thriving feel stifling, boring, outdated, uncomfortable, or downright unbearable until you do the right thing and move on.

The place I turned to next was getting a Master's Degree in Spiritual Psychology to try and sort through all of the madness. It was not until years of therapy, deep dives into processing, thousands of dollars invested in life/business coaching, hundreds of books later, that I found out that I am an Undefined Solar Plexus in Human Design. This little key piece of knowledge pretty much handled all the pain and drama within one year of finding out about how these Undefined Centers and my Aura Type operate. (Don't worry, I will get to this soon and wipe off a decade of therapy for you too!)

But, that is not to discount all I learned in therapy and getting my Master's Degree. It was crucial to begin the journey of healing, and I needed a lot of that. Healing is a deep soothing balm to relax the traumas, the dreams unfulfilled, the betrayals, the being taken down from the Projection pedestal and driven out of town, all of the madness. To let go and redefine yourself. It takes self-care, healing, time, and the ability to awaken in the moment without looking back. A lot of forgiveness to yourself for everything you did that hurt others and, of course, forgiving everyone who hurt you. If you have had cavernous past abuse or trauma, supplementing any tools with spiritual therapy can be such a gift to heal past wounds. This time of self-nurture, deep alone time, reflection was incredibly wonderful for me.

When I left San Francisco, I made an inner vow: the commitment was TO BE OF SERVICE. I came to this profound internal pledge because going after superficial dreams with such gusto created absolutely no inner gratification. It was ego serving and quite painful. Very shallow relationships and experiences, and for me in San Francisco, it was embarrassing, really. The puffed-up egos, when my mission was soulful, I was on a vision quest. I was a spiritual practitioner, but this was unnoticed and definitely not valued by any of my community at the time. Of course, why should anyone have? I was doing spiritual work in a rock world? Quite a conundrum that made no sense, but it indeed was magical for those few who did recognize it.

So, I chose to walk away and seek something more meaningful. When I stumbled upon this opportunity with this corporate company, I rode the wave. The interesting thing was they were on the upward surge, and I surfed it. But, if you know anything about franchising, the fall is also swift if you grow too fast. I luckily did not experience the fall. I was there in the glory days and loved every minute of it.

So, this brings you up to speed with the backdrop. Why this is so important, most of my clients are in some way deep on their spiritual journey or have read every self-help book. Maybe you have too?

They have maybe mastered many tools or have done years of therapy as I did. Yet there was still something missing. Or they had invested thousands on high-end coaching with coaches who did not really see them. So, I wanted to share the depth of looking and exploration I had done. Yet although the tools were excellent, they missed some severe critical insights for me. Human Design is still a very new tool; I believe a very advanced upgraded information that is absolutely needed for humanity to ease through these changing times. It is still information that hasn't hit the mainstream. It is reserved for a small percentage of the population willing to see themselves. The reason for this is, meeting this intel unravels everything you thought you knew about who you are. Also, where this intel really hits people is for anyone who has clients of any kind: coaches, therapists, business mentors, even influencers. If you don't know the uniqueness of the people you are serving, and why 90% of your clientele doesn't get any results with your tools, you must take this knowledge seriously if you don't want your business to be obsolete in a few years. No offense, but I hope the crash and burn is grueling for those coaches who are Manifestors or Manifesting Generators and are charging high-end prices just to shame their unique following for not getting results with the methods that worked for them. Enough already. We need an upgrade in the self-help coaching industry!

I absolutely felt like I had seen it all, tried it all, and still suffered. That is very painful, so it might help you if you've ever said to yourself, "I've tried everything, and nothing works." So perhaps you can trust me that this knowledge I will reveal to you is quite different. Also, this is my great intention for anyone who may be experiencing these words right now. This is much more than cocktail talk or intellectual musings. The true power comes when your inner conviction says, "I will commit to trying the experiment – to living it." So, once you make this commitment, give yourself at least three months, seven years is better, but you have to start somewhere.

Once you make this commitment, reading the rest of this will have an even more profound impact. The commitment you are making is experimenting with your personal Strategy for your Type and your unique inner decision-making process for literal decisions in your life. If you make this commitment, let us know! We want to hear from you and hear about your journey, your experiences. We have a thriving community of people taking on the experiment, built just for that, so join us there so we can swim in the waters with you as you dive in! Just go to our website and grab our bonus PDF materials just for those who are reading this book:

https://foxy5d.com/pages/are-you-a-mutant

Chapter 4

Figuring Out the Money Thing

All of us are living with dogmas that we accept as truths. When one of these is overturned, there is an initial gasp, soon followed by a rush of exhilaration.
Deepak Chopra

So, I had been working for this company for a while. I had also bought and sold one of the stores and made a great return on investment. The corporate office hired me to oversee the entire Southern California, Arizona, and Nevada regions. I was flying worldwide; I did training with hundreds of women as the brand and company grew. I loved it for a long time. Until the boredom set in, the discomfort, that nagging ache that you knew you were born for something more. You know the time when you start getting incredibly dissatisfied with the workload, the people, the corporate brainwashing, the burnout. This company motivated by fear; you don't perform, you lose your job type of pressure. So, the conditioning and Penta created an intense groove of anxiety. I knew it was time to leave. But how? What was next?

Very scary, very confusing; I did not know what the next path was.

I wanted an online career but being seen was so excruciatingly painful from my previous experience in San Francisco that I decided to do something else. Also, in my fear Gates, I have the Fear of the Past and the Fear of the Future. So, that makes for a lot of stuckness, along with my Individuality. So, I was stuck for a long time. One day in yoga class, I got an idea that stuck with me: to buy a juice bar, and I went out and manifested it. I pushed and pushed and made it happen.

Now, if you couldn't tell from the tone of this last sentence, this strategy is the one you know everyone is taught: get a brilliant idea in the shower, walking, or at a yoga class (wherever ideas are sold to you) and go out and make it happen. The only thing I knew to do and did with just about everything in my life.

Well, this strategy will only work for an exceedingly small percentage of the population. Let us just say, I am NOT one of them. According to this intel, only between 8-9% of the population should get an idea, take action, and will ultimately have success with it. Some will, and those people will have significant results. As a matter of fact, most of them are the population that built a lot of the world we now live in. They trained us that this is the way to reach your goals.

So, most of us push and shove, force, hustle and emit a huge amount of toxicity into the world through our frustration, bitterness, and disappointment when it all falls to shit like it so violently did for me after I bought this juice bar.

So, back to the story. I bought a brick-and-mortar raw vegan juice bar in the middle of WeHo (West Hollywood, CA), thinking this would be a good investment for passive income.

I also got a promotion with corporate at this time with a sister company. It was a different focus, and I thought maybe this was the way out. But instead, I ended up taking the promotion and running this juice bar in West Hollywood. Now, this is where my life takes a turn for the absolute very worse.

It was during this time, Davidian, my then very new BF, now life and business partner, who is designed to mutate the path of others, introduced me to the fact that I am a Projector in Human Design. Mutate my path he did – and big time. Not a very convenient time to find this out. When I was working full time and running a raw vegan juice bar in the busiest part of the world with 15 20-something employees and a 3-hour commute both ways. SCREAM FACE EMOJI!

I was about to fast-track my Human Design experiment, and

I suffered, but I also learned so much. I learned do not ever initiate if you are a Projector. Do not ever work 12-hour days, do not commute on the 405, and most importantly, do not ever get an idea and go out there and make it happen. Your brain may be so fried right now, like what do you mean that doesn't work?

That is what we are taught to do consistently, and there is no questioning the validity of this approach. It is just something we all do. Just like Nike says, Just Do it! We all look up to that billboard, stare up onto that shiny dogma and say, "Yes, I can do it!" Please take a deep sigh of relief because, as you read this book, I am going to share with you exactly who can manifest this way and who cannot, and why. Then you will feel like a vast 5,000 pound boulder will be removed from your shoulders, and you will finally be able to relax and live as you were designed to. I have not met one person, unless they really do not know their birth time or are incredibly seeped in their NOT-SELF theme, saying that this intel didn't nail them accurately. Well, not true, I do see some people who have gained success as their Not-Self theme who are attached to these outward results; and they don't want to unravel a thing. Also, for some people, this intel is just not designed for them, and they are not interested. Or, for some people heavily invested in a belief system, challenging what they believe in is just too much for their rooted establishment. If you are here and drawn to this knowledge, you will most likely be transformed by the experiment. As you continue to read on, trust me on following the experiment, try out your unique Strategy. You will know precisely what never to do again.

So yeah, I learned that as a Projector (and one of the first things you hear about this is): you don't want to get yourself in a position where you are giving over 12 hours a day to work; you will quickly frazzle out all your circuits. This is precisely what happened to me. I would come home crying, couldn't think, had one emergency after the next; my brain couldn't process. It was pure chaos.

So, the first thing I did was quit the extremely high-pressured six-figured position. I thought the juice bar was the exit strategy, but it was more like the how can I quickly crumble my life to a halt strategy and get massively into debt, burn myself out, cry tirelessly on the bathroom floor, and basically leave with nothing, strategy.

So, you could imagine the stress of the juice bar; the store opened at 6am and closed at 8pm PST, and I had 15 employees all in their 20s.

I had to commute on the 405 during rush hour, which is every hour, so basically, I got no sleep. I had employees stealing from me, calling in sick, shutting down the store, doing all kinds of shenanigans. So, to discover you are a Projector and the light shines on why this is so violently wrong for you, you feel relief and like… oh fuck… at the same time. Like this little piece of intel is going to just bring the whole house crashing and burning down to the ground. Particularly if you are in the Quarter of Transformation (Mutation), and you have Channel 25-51, the Channel of Shock. That is exactly as it sounds! So, don't worry if these Human Design terms are throwing you off; this is preciously what this book is all about. I will break it all down as we go and share how you can also navigate life, business, and your life purpose through the lens of Human Design. But some of you who already know these terms will have a good chuckle to yourself. These markers clearly show why I went through such a shocking transformation when I found out I was a Projector.

The reason it took me so long to accept I was a Projector? Yes, I heard the term about a year before it integrated into my psyche. But I denied it for so long because the material was so complicated and intellectually written that I just couldn't relate to the intel. I kept saying to myself, I am such a major Manifestor, and this intel is ridiculous. So, it was Davidian that was the Human Design whisperer; he introduced the knowledge to me and brought me to a couple of things super clear about what I was going through, and it was mind-altering.

So spoiler alert – just because you might not be a "Manifestor" in Human Design does not mean you are not here to be a kick-ass Manifestor in life – it just means you have a different strategy to manifest your dreams.

The strategies on manifesting a life correctly, and all the explanations, will be explained in this book. I am placing it alongside my journey, so hopefully, it gives you hope that you too (regardless of any crazy life pandemonium you may have experienced) can learn how to manifest. Even if you are NOT a "Manifestor." Another spoiler alert – most Manifestors are so conditioned out of being the lions they were born to be that they are hiding out in society as imploded sheep not manifesting anything. Sad but true. So we all have been through some suffering, so stay with me through this book step by step, and I will give you a free pass out of the torture!

It hit me like a stabbing in the heart, the insights about being a Projector. You try to do things like other people, but it doesn't work out the same way for you. You have so much to say about what others need and would have success if only they could hear you. But they don't listen, they ignore you, or worse yet, they steal your ideas, take them for themselves without giving you any credit. Your thoughts get stolen, you create things, but people just take them, not honoring what you have created.

So, this happened to me over and over and over again. Even at the juice bar, I developed my own product line, YUP, labels, and all. It was a superfoods replacement for coffee. Another juice bar opened across the street (literally selling a line of the same type of products I had created with different labels). Yes, seriously, it was following me like a curse.

Sure, I manifested success in my twenties, but I was f-ing bitter.

I could not understand why I would be unrecognized as the

one who breathed the life force into this group. It all birthed from my living room in my house, but no one believed I was the group's founder. It wasn't me who started the group, and of course, I didn't protect myself legally. Everyone said it was this person or that person that made it successful. Do you know how many times I have heard this before?

How the group in San Francisco just stole the material and made a career of it for the next decade, even though our lawyer said they would have to pay me for any of the work they did. Yes, bitter, a wee bit bitter until it all came crumbling down, down, down.

I screamed louder, I demanded more adamantly, but I was in so much pain. Bitterness is too light a description when you have been living the NOT-SELF THEME for so long, and you are in more pain than you can explain. Nothing works, you're burned out, you are exhausted, but you have just run a 10k marathon and are still broke, and you don't know what to do next, your bills are piling up. You may have accrued credit card debt, mine was over 80k (today, I am happy to say I am 100% debt-free), and then you reach a breaking point where you cannot work another day, and the debtors are coming after you with fury. Your Generator and Manifesting Generators are looking down their nose at you. Haven't you learned your lesson with credit card debt yet? You want to scream at every Generator in this world who can survive this lunacy and tell them to take this credit card system and shove it where the sun doesn't shine. It is quite literally excruciating. You just completed a decade of therapy and processing. You have done hours of forgiveness, healing the wounded inner child, letting go of all who betrayed you and those you may have betrayed as well, but still, the bitterness aggressively burns the mouth, soul, and psyche.

So, when I began to hear the description of the Human Design Projector, I knew this SHIT WAS GOOD. Whatever Ra Uru Hu (the founder of Human Design) was smoking, he downloaded

EPIC, I mean 100% epic intel. Never in my life – after reading everything I have studied – have I found a system that blows my mind over and over and over again.

It gets deeper and deeper with each layer, and my job is to mutate the entire tribe with this intel and bring it to my unique fractal in a simple way you can immediately GET IT, but also in a way that just might shock you into your own life transformation.

My grandest intention for anyone reading this is to know that there is a way out regardless of the turmoil you may find yourself in right now. If a job or career might be bleeding you dry, if you feel you are designed for something new, once you learn your Strategy, it will begin to open new doors for you in a brand NEW WAY!

Inspiring people to live it is magical because that is the real turn-on. The toaster oven just doesn't work until you plug it into the electricity, and once you do, the heat amps up miraculously. This is the only way with this intel; it is living intelligence. It exists in each one of us in our unique way. What I can do for you is say look at what happened to me, but then look inside you and watch it turn on. Watch that acorn crack open and sprout and witness the oak tree start making roots. It will never turn on the same way in one person as it does in another. There will never be a blueprint for success that everyone can follow. You will need to feel it, live it, let it unfold inside of you. It's alive; it either works for you, or it doesn't. So, don't believe me, or doubt what I am saying or try to discredit these words; just try it on for yourself. If your life gets better, what have you to lose? If your life stays the same, then maybe this is not intel for you.

So, I found out I was a Projector, and once I hit extreme burnout and there was nowhere to go, I surrendered. I quit the job, sold the juice bar, and slept in. Ha, that was nice; having no idea how I would support myself was not fun. It did not take me long before I just surrendered this journey and began to live my Design. Everyone said to me, you must go into the store. You cannot just let it fall apart. But I did; I just let it go. It was to the point I could not get out of bed. Luckily, I could sell the store at the final hour (barely), but I still walked away burned out, fried, unable to hear another blender, beat up, and in serious debt. With absolutely no idea what to do next, no way of making a living, no career, and no inspiration or direction on the next step. Just an FYI, the store is a successful brand juice bar and is still doing great in the country; it just wasn't RIGHT for me at that time.

So, back to sleeping in! I began creating a nice slow day, long morning teas, luxurious walks, studying Human Design, long baths, all day starting to live as a Projector. And it felt like heaven instantaneously.

I said, this is it. I am taking it on. I am living this and believing what they say that if you are designed to be a Projector, it will work out, and you will be led – if you follow your Strategy and Inner Authority – to a life that reflects who you truly are. I f-ing took this seriously. As you know, at this point, I had courses, degrees, certifications, books on so many things, not just Shamanism, Spiritual Psychology, but also many forms of manifestation, Science of Mind (avid Agape goer), reiki, meditation, channeling, self-help galore, EFT, Epigenetics, energy healing, tarot, Akashic Records, past life regressions, motivational tools, business gurus – I studied A LOT OF STUFF. So, when I say the news that I am a Projector literally shook my world to its core and explained my entire life plight, it is saying a ton. So, if it nailed me so unbelievably perfectly, I decided I had no other choice. I'm jumping in the water, diving in the dark sea, no buoy or safety raft, I'm going IN deep.

But this path takes courage and the Strategy. It sounds so simple, but it is a lot more challenging than it sounds. I was scared shitless to live as a Projector; it felt so helpless. But everything I had tried in the past was excruciating; I knew I had to try something different. I knew I was going to be OK. Even though every business I had started in the past drained me, and I wanted to stay with a guaranteed corporate salary, I knew I was on the right path.

I had a sense that learning I was a Projector was a minor mini-inner tsunami that was filling me up in tidal wave fashion. I knew that I would upend every single concept of myself and rearrange it all until I was ultimately a new person.

This was precisely what happened, but it took some time and study.

So, then what... What does a Projector do next, you ask?

WAIT.

And...

Wait.

And... Wait. And OMFG, am I really going to wait when I have no income? Then you wait some more. That is when the mind goes bat-shit crazy, and this is when the wheat separates from the chaff. Or the warriors of the intel emerge, and those giving it lip service go back and get a job, or panic, or whatever. There is nothing wrong with going back and working. I did it SEVERAL, SEVERAL, SEVERAL TIMES! Before my own business really took off, I applied and got several different at-home-type jobs. You do what you have to do until the pathway finally lights up. This is when we surrender to the power of living as our true selves. I did not take this study intending to teach this stuff; I did it to survive and thrive in my life. So, I just followed my S&IA (Strategy and Inner Authority). My mind thought, "Oh, I am designed to be a Spiritual business coach, this makes sense. I trained women in my Corporate career in their businesses," so I would act on that for a while. Business coaches would say, yes, you have to do it this way, approach your friends for clients, and create this launch. My mind would say, "That worked for them, and I need to make money, so all these approaches sounded good," until I tried, and those ideas just wouldn't work out for me. After years of studying this intel, finally, my mind slowly began to let go, and I waited for the right invitations to come in, and this was the INITIATION of this work (LIVING IT), and this was the direction the invitations led me.

Now, please note that the mind is a wild and crazy beast.

So, I incorporated A LOT OF TOOLS that finally started to work for me that never worked in the past. These tools finally worked because I integrated all my past knowledge and synthesized it distinctly in specific terms based on my Design. The Law of Attraction never worked when conditioned as a Generator because I would have a download take action and fail epically, so I got bitter none of that shit worked.

But here, as a Projector now in the waiting – I could see how the tools could assist with the mind.

Instead of initiating, I visualized, did the energy work, and created a parallel reality in my mind. All this could be done in bed, and that was a good thing for a burned-out Projector. Because after I sold the juice bar and quit the corporate thing, I pretty much needed to sleep for a year. LOL. So anything you can do while crashed-out recuperating is a good thing.

So let's dive into the intel. By now, you should have your free chart, so allow me to begin with the basics on how to read your chart. If you don't have your free chart, you can grab it on our accompanying PDF: https://foxy5d.com/pages/are-you-a-mutant.

An important caveat here! As I am exploring the themes and information in Human Design, it is essential to remember that the founder of Human Design stated over and over that this information was for everyone! That not one person had the market on this intel, that we were all here to mutate the information for the evolution of humanity. He knew that everyone would experiment with this information and bring forward something unique for others to glean from after the experiment. After the founder transitioned for the sake of business, many people purport that they have the best knowledge or the insider ability to pass on this information. NOT TRUE... not true. You are allowed to learn from the people you are inspired to learn from. This knowledge is here for us to LIVE and experiment with until it practically guides each person individually. If you are following a tribal system and you can't live for yourself, think for yourself, or run your entrepreneurial enterprise in your way, this is a malfunction of a tribal Human Design rulership. My job is to bust out of this tribal control, mutate the intel, lead, guide, and direct this new transformation based on MY INNER AUTHORITY, and provide the intel based on my journey.

I am not asking you to believe me. This is from my own journey and experience with the intel. It is unique and solely based on my profoundly spiritual development and life background. I have been through the crucible and experimented with this knowledge; it worked for me; it radically changed my life and many of the lives of my clients. So, controlling what I am saying or how I am running my business is actually a betrayal to the very system you are purporting to live by. Talk about irony. So, take what you resonate with and move on if this intel is not for you.

Chapter 5

Chart Reading Basics

If you allow someone to be who they are and they allow you to be who you are, then that's love. Anything else is torture.
Ra Uru Hu

Before we go into your unique Type, I want to give you the basics of reading your chart. When you first look at your chart, it can feel super confusing and overwhelming, so I want to break it down for you in a simple process to understand and implement it. Again, what separates this knowledge is experimenting with it, not "learning" it.

So, understanding what you are looking at will give you the leaping-off point! Grab your chart. Here are some of the elements we will be looking at in this book:

Your Type:

- You will either be a Manifestor, Generator, Manifesting Generator (SubType of Generator but operates very uniquely), Projector, or a Reflector.
- Your Signature: Peace, Satisfaction, Success, or Awe. The Signature is the feeling you have when you are operating correctly as yourself 😊 ahhh, we love this one!

Your Strategy:

- This is your unique Strategy to lead you to live in your Signature Theme. Your Strategy will be either: To Inform, Wait to Respond, Wait for the Invitation, or Wait for a Lunar Cycle. Do not stress; I will explain these in detail

29

when I go through each Type.

Inner Authority:

- Inner Authority: You will either be Emotional, Sacral, Splenic, Ego, Self-Projected, Mental/None, Lunar Authority. I will go into this in more depth as well. This is what we call your INNER GPS System. This is how you learn to follow your Inner Authority, and you are led to the right life, right people, the right career, right direction, proper purpose.

Definition:

- Definition: You will see this as either Single, Split Definition, Triple Split, or Quadruple Split. I will go through the basics of what this means, particularly when it comes to business.

Profile:

- Profile: There are 12 different Profiles, and this will look like 1/3, 1/4, 2/4, 2/5, 3/5, 3/6, 4/6, 4/1, 5/1, 5/2, 6/2, 6/3. Your Profile is much like the costume you wear in the world. We will not go too deeply into this here in this book, but will have more in the accompanying PDF.

9 Centers:

- There are nine Centers, the Crown (Head), Ajna, Throat, Ego (Heart/Will), G-Center, Spleen, Solar Plexus (Emotional Center), Sacral, and Root. The Centers are the areas in your chart that look like the Chakra system. They are different shapes and different colors. The only thing to contemplate here is whether the Center is colored in or white, and in Chapter 14 I will take you through the power journey of discovering the magic of these Centers through this new lens.

The idea of Human Design, putting it simply: use your personal Strategy and your personal GPS system to move out of your Not-Self theme and into your Signature theme.

And then, all of humanity can live happily ever after. Yes, truly, it is that simple. Of course, you have to overcome your mind telling you that it is bat-shizz crazy and nothing could be that easy. Then, of course, you have to allow others to live exactly as their unique self. This idea would need to include people who make a lot of money or make the world go round using other people. So they would also have to be willing to give up control of others, which is much easier said than done. But after that, then yup, it's that easy, happily ever after for all of humanity at large. Mic drop!

Now that we know how effortless this can all be, the chart can also be infinitely complex. Very similar to fractal geometry in this concept, super simple and yet infinitely complex as well as self-similar. So, no matter where you begin looking, you will see yourself.

When you look at your chart, you will see on the left side red numbers, and on the right, you see black numbers. You will see these black and red half-lines and complete lines, some candy-striped red and black. A half-line is called a Hanging Gate; when it is the complete line, it is called a Channel. Each one of these Gates correlates to the I Ching. Each Gate and Channel is a deep dive into another piece of who you are. It is said the I Ching correlates to the DNA code. Both the I Ching and the DNA are codes. It is said that not only do they use the same code,

but the same alphabet, they actually speak the same language and if they were to exchange information, would understand each other perfectly. Martin Schonberger, a German scientist who wrote the book *The I Ching & the Genetic Code*, recently discovered that the two Codons which contain the genetic-chemical message "to stop" have the same numeric structure of the hexagram 63, After Completion, and the Codons which, so to speak, act to say "Go" on a genetic level, correspond to the opposite hexagram 64, Before Completion. In the DNA they serve as punctuation between code sequences. In the I Ching, we have hexagrams #63 and #64 which serve the same purpose.

From the blog *Thoughts of a Taoist Babe*, https://taobabe.rocks/about-me/

In Human Design, the I Ching makes up the Gates, and the intel of each Gate is written in a new type of code based on the I Ching system to understand who you are. Human Design combines ancient mystery school teachings, the Kabbalah, the I Ching, the Chakra System, Astrology, and modern-day sciences, including Epigenetics and quantum physics. The chart is a composite of all of humanity and the experiences contained therein. The aspects you have colored in, either red/black or one of the Centers colored in, are places that make up who you are, something that is consistent within you. The white areas are energies you probably understand. The energies move through you, but often they are not really yours; you pick them up but usually distort and blow the frequency out of proportion.

These white or Undefined areas in your chart are inconsistent; they represent where you are taking in the outside world, being CONDITIONED into something you are not. When you are operating out of this NOT-SELF theme, you will find yourself in a great deal of pain. So, the intention of discovering who you are and what you can rely on, and what is not you, is to ultimately free yourself from suffering. Anyone else here had enough and are DONE WITH the suffering? Just send me a little amen, sister. I hear you through the multidimensional time and space grid. This brings me to the last piece you will see when you get your free basic chart, probably one of the most critical pieces to this intel.

The Not-Self Theme:

- Not-Self Theme – You will either see: Anger, Frustration, Bitterness, or Disappointment. These are the feelings within you that amplify when you are living as your Not-Self.

The Not-Self theme means that when you live based on your conditioning by the world, these feelings will monopolize your experiences in life. So, in other words, if you follow the rule of your parents, your teachers, your gurus, your priests, your community, to live a certain way without ever really asking, "Is this really what I want?" you will probably have a deep-down sense of this Not-Self theme. This theme is the primary energy you will feel when living out of the Not-Self energy. When you are conditioned, you take on other people's energy, you think it is YOU, then you amplify it, you distort it, and then you live as this Not-Self energy. You believe it is you and take action from this distorted perception, and unfortunately, it makes you feel super angry, frustrated, bitter, or disappointed, depending on which Type you are. You have a unique relationship with the Not-Self theme. It is an overwhelming energy that permeates your consciousness even if you have reached your goals – not all achievements are alike. You see, taking action or achieving goals in a way that is not correct for you causes more pain than joy. If you have ever landed a dream job, house, career, relationship that you always wanted but were suffering more deeply than ever before once you got it, you understand what I mean by this. Now, of course, we all feel every one of these Not-Self themes from time to time. However, you will feel a special relationship with your Type's theme. So for Manifestors, it is anger, and often there is a repressed rage in these people that is palpable. Generators will feel frustration; you can see this when someone is working in an office they hate, and every daily task is wrought with frustration. A Projector will have a unique relationship with bitterness – as I explained from my own life, just bitter that everything is so much harder for us. We might be the most intelligent or most aware people in the room, but no one sees us. The Reflector is disappointed in all they see with humanity in general. Just a sense that being around people or having any friends is overrated and disappointing.

Chapter 6

Human Design Types

As for you, my beloved friend, I loyally believe in your uniqueness; but whenever I try to tell to you wherein it consists, I helplessly describe only a type.
Josiah Royce

What a great quote to start this chapter, because each person is infinitely complex and unique, as we learn in Human Design, but we simplify it down to start, with 4 Types. Then we reveal the layers upon layers to unravel the complexities that only your Design will have. For example, each Gate will have a line number, a Base, a Tone, and a Color. So even if you share the same Gate with another person, it becomes infinitely more complex if you have a differing line, located in a particular planetary influence. Then you will probably have a differing Base, Tone, Color. Each Gate has over 1,000 variations. So yes we are all infinitely different and unique. However, the place we start is your Type! By Type, we are referring to your Aura Type. There are four different Aura Types.

So, the first place to begin is with, what is your Aura Type? (Great new pick-up line at a bar!) And with this Aura Type, you have a special code to crack the unique way it was designed to operate in the world.

This Strategy based on the Type is your personal Success Code. This code is only good FOR YOU!

Once you master your Success Code or Strategy, you will then understand you also have an extraordinary Inner Authority, which we refer to as your GPS System. When you follow this, it will help you make decisions that are right for you.

This decision-making process will align you to the right

choice, the right life purpose, the right direction, and yes, even to the riches most people often long for. Only instead of reaching some goal that's devoid of inner satisfaction when you reach your success, you will feel aligned, satisfied, in awe of the world, rather than empty, burned-out, or disappointed with what you got.

You are all now familiar with my backstory: at the very peak of success with the Performance Band, I was in the worst pain. We performed in front of 10k people. Magic Johnson and Sharon Stone introduced us to the crowd. *The Hedwig and the Angry Inch* cast were also performing with us. I felt we were at the pinnacle of "success." However, my band members were so loud and obnoxious in the dressing room, snorting drugs and screaming, and they were so under my skin. When you are in a group with only 12 other people, you are in like a wickedly complicated incestuous community marriage. I was so unseen, unrecognized, and no one GOT me. It was torture.

Well, I have to say, looking back on it, one person saw me, and this soul sister BFF witness saved me. She and I created the Vortex, a studio for events, rehearsals, and a place to live. This journey with her was truly magical and still is! We continue to create, travel, laugh, explore life together. So, having a few people who SEE you as a Projector is enormous. You may only have five aligned people who genuinely recognize you throughout your life, which will be a saving grace. She recognized me as the visionary leader and saw me as the spiritual radical visionary teacher that I was. Our joy creating and living together in San Francisco rescued me during a time when so many were on the attack. Not knowing I was a Line 5 about to be burned at the stake by the community, gruesome details for another time. Having one person hold me up and love me through success and failure is a true sacred friendship. I will always be forever grateful.

But, there is no denying I was the least happy I had ever felt inside, at the height of my success. Achieving this monumental goal, most people only dream of, through pushing, scratching, clawing, and striving your way to the top tactics. It is excruciating. It all looks good on the outside to most people; however, it is often rotting on the inside. We see this repeatedly with our most successful artists, directors, musicians, politicians, or business owners. They may have achieved great accolades, but their lives are wrought with corruption, affairs, depression, drug or other addictions, drama, and abuse. We have watched many suicides, yet we still strive for things based on the façade rather than our inner compass.

For me, I didn't understand much at that time. Although I was getting a lot of outer accolades, and so many people were jealous, something was off, big time, inside of me.

How could achieving these outside accolades bring me so much pain and suffering? I was not using manifestation tools in the right way. It was SOOO confusing. I had manifested everything I wanted, but I was miserable, as I am sure so many people understand who are striving and reaching goals they thought would bring them happiness. I was in so much treacherous pain. I had to figure out how to heal my life! Leaving the group at the height of this career caused pain to the entire company. I know people dedicated themselves to this vision. To this day, many of the members, those who I gave a foundation for their whole careers, still hate me. I didn't understand my behavior at this point, but when the pain reached its crucible, I just left it all behind, let it blow up in smoke, and I walked away from it all. I am not proud of how it was all handled, still in my 20s and addicted to drama. I have in the past felt an incredible amount of guilt, sadness, and loss over the experience. Whether they hate me or not, each of these members still holds a powerful and sacred place in my heart. But, when you are in that level of pain, you have to cut loose. There is no other choice; at least for me, there was not. So, instead of suffering at this peak of success, I cut myself loose and had to leave. Needless to say, it was traumatic for everyone involved.

After the healing journey, I had to understand what happened in terms of my unique Aura Type creating many of these circumstances – from this perspective: it was NOT PERSONAL. It was mechanical. Had I known my Design, none of this would have happened in this fashion.

Part of my intention for bringing out this intel is because it saved my life. Understanding my past in these terms explained everything. If we all operated as ourselves and started with the premise that we are all unique and need different ways to operate, most people would live extraordinarily more satisfying lives. I would have never pushed harder, strived more vehemently to achieve my vision had I known about being a Projector, the minute people tried to claim the rights to my vision, or say I was not the creator of the group, or the person who created the entire foundation to honor each person. The foundation was established to actually allow each person to be autonomous and not be controlled by the leader. I wanted this in my work which is the gift I gave. Most of them took this to mean they created the group; it was theirs to do with it what they wanted. Now, I see through my Design. I would have known, "Oh, these people don't recognize me, move on. You are not seen here; let's seek another way to unleash your genius. You are a Line 5 being Projected on; they might spend their whole life bashing you, so please move on." Instead, I bathed in a sea of bloody self-torture porn, screaming for recognition to an audience of blind people until my voice collapsed. It was a gruesome decade.

So with these tools, you might learn how to achieve success in a wonderfully awe-inspiring way. Rather than the torture I went through. So, with that introduction, you should know, when you learn your Aura, you align to not just the "success" that is deemed outstanding by the outside accolades of the world, but inner harmonies that just might have eluded you without the knowledge. *So, first things first, show me your chart.* Let's get into it! BTW this is our most favorite T-shirt quote! You might come to understand, as we have, that knowing each other's chart is an incredibly nourishing and supportive way to honor the people in your life and give everyone in your community the freedom to be seen and acknowledged for their uniqueness. So, let's normalize revealing your chart before working together, dating, or conducting any type of business!

Your Aura Mechanics Are Unique To You!

Now we are ready to give you the manual to your personalized GPS system! Your unique Aura and the correct success Strategy FOR YOU.

Yes, some people will have similarities at first glance, but this is the art of differentiation, so the further down you look at a chart, the more unique you get. Color/Base/Tone, many contributing factors make each human individual. Now, the idea is learning your differences, honoring your differences, letting everyone off the hook, and giving them the free pass to leave the tribal dinner table to BE THEMSELVES without the guilt and stink eye.

So let's discuss what the Aura is. I know the study of Aura has been nebulous at best, and those who see them talk about colors and shapes and different changes with frequency shifts and can make this talk about Auras confusing.

In this system, we evaluate different Auras based on Type and look at this energy very differently from the glowing colors around your body. The Aura can be metaphorically viewed as your spaceship moving you through time, space in the dimension of your physical body: your own little ship bubble moving through space.

It reaches out about two arm lengths from your body forward, up, out, and behind you. It is the nonverbal communication that speaks between people without words. It is what is being said as you walk into a room without you ever opening your mouth.

If you have ever felt like you understood someone from them just walking in the room, the narcissist, the belle of the ball, the fighter, the bashful one, the sense of someone without even an introduction, then you understand the essence of Aura.

Each Aura needs the other Aura Types to succeed and thrive in this world. The short explanation, we need each other, we are not here (none of us) to operate alone. Yet, if we don't recognize each person for the unique way they work in the world and let each person BE WHO THEY ARE, we ALL SUFFER.

Sounds simple enough? Know who you are, act as YOURSELF, and let others be themselves.

Everyone let out a sigh of relief now altogether!

Alright, let's move on.

I will teach you some essential core tools to find your way in the world with this knowledge.

So, by now, you know I am a Splenic Projector (you will all learn more about your Type and what it means below). I have a unique Auric field, and I need to operate in a cool way. (Any of you who know what it is to be a Projector, this is my very nice way of saying we don't quite fit into the modern-day world yet, and it's not fun.) Not to say we are not designed to work or run businesses, because we are. We are here to run businesses from a leadership position and open the world up to a brand-new way to work. The caveat is we need the rest of the world to understand this so we can all thrive. Hence why I am so called to get this intel to more people. We all awaken into our superpower genius as each person is recognized for their genius and allowed to play their part correctly.

As Projectors, we need to operate in work that is different from 80% of the population. AH, relief, I finally get to be me. You finally get to be YOU! I really cannot completely express the pain I have felt most of my life trying to fit into a world that was not designed for my Type. You see, this is still a Generator world. (Our time has not yet come but is almost here! The

Projector is here to lead this mutation, so the time is soon for this Projector Type to be recognized.) Oh, I wanted so badly to be heard and seen that it ached, not just seen but understood as myself. The pain was so desperate I can only tell you that when I found out the truth of my Aura, my unique Strategy and way to live, and I was different, I had the most significant AHA moment of my life.

Now, it is time for you to be you and fulfill your destiny on this earth. You are being led here for a reason, you have synchronistically found these pages, and you probably wish for a new way. Regardless of your age, literally, at any age, you can begin to live in a WHOLE NEW way as yourself.

We are moving into the ERA OF THE INDIVIDUAL. This has to do with the shifting of the wheel. I will explain this in great depth shortly, so we can all prepare for these coming times together.

If you don't find out who you are and operate as yourself, you might feel a little angry, frustrated, extremely resentful, and bitter, just plain disappointed that you don't have what you wanted already in life. Or confused why you aren't happy when you do achieve your goals or, worse yet, simply stymied about the state of the world we are in, not knowing where to turn for meaning and truth.

So, relax; all you need do is NOT *BELIEVE* ME. Just try this out for yourself. EXPERIMENT. If it works, wow, a life you were meant to live begins to unfold with grace and ease. And if it fails, you get more of what you have now, no harm done.

So let's get into it. There are four Types of Auras, You can be:

1. Manifestor
2. Generator (Includes Manifesting Generator)
3. Projector
4. Reflector

Knowing your Type allows you to understand your Not-Self theme and your perfect Strategy. In other words, it shows you when you are off course or when you are moving towards your life purpose, meaning when you are ON COURSE! Navigating by the energy of your Signature Theme means it is always directing you towards how you will manifest with the LEAST amount of resistance. We all want to live a life in alignment with our true life purpose; ultimately, we all have the human desire to fulfill our destiny and play our role in this extraordinary game here on life school earth. However, there is SO MUCH confusion, conditioning, propaganda on what to do, how to do it, what way to live that we have forgotten HOW to be ourselves. Our minds are so inundated with thoughts about what we should do, and it speaks with our voice and memories that we mistakenly think OUR MIND IS WHO WE ARE. Breathe in with me here for a moment to contemplate.

According to Human Design, listen in to this very carefully. The mind and its ongoing running monologues are simply the conditioning of the planet, the matrix, the family, the schools, the teachers, the parents speaking to us; it is NOT US. It is who you think you are, but it is NOT THE TRUTH of who you are. Read that again. The beauty of Human Design is once you understand this, we can show you exactly where you have taken on other people's indoctrination and life force energy THAT WAS **NOT** YOU.

Now, this sounds confusing; I get it. But wouldn't you like to rest into the energy that is meant for you to excel with and let go of the onslaught of energies that are dragging you into anger, bitterness, and frustration? Don't pause; the answer to this rhetorical question is an astounding yes, please. Simply put, with a little trust and investigation, you get to release the STUFF that is keeping you from your BLISS.

So now, I mean, seriously, NOW, I am putting the power of you back in your hands.

YOUR RULING FORCE IS YOUR STRATEGY AND YOUR INNER AUTHORITY. You cannot look to a teacher, guru, or coach to make decisions for you ever again! YOU RULE YOUR OWN DECISION-MAKING. YOU GOT THE POWER. Your decision-making process also needs to be taken out of the hands of your annoying MIND CHATTER, to be put into your unique Inner Authority and Strategy.

You already committed to experimenting here and not just taking my word for it. So, even though it sounds oh so, super simple – it is genuinely NOT EASY.

Take out your chart, look under where it says **Type** and contemplate the below information:

1. Manifestors

So, for those Manifestors: You are here to know peace; if you feel anger, you are in the middle of your Not-Self theme. Your strategy is TO INFORM. So, what does that mean? Yes, you are here to manifest and take action and initiate at the rate of informing all of those you will impact. You might feel like you are in a hurry, moving faster than everyone around you; however, if you do not inform, you will piss people off, have manifestations that don't stick and be angry at yourself and others (A LOT). You might feel like, "I don't have time to tell people, I am in a hurry, I have to get this done, telling people slows me down. Trying to explain what I am up to is excruciating for me; I just do it." These are some sentences that express how some Manifestors might feel. Informing is most definitely not natural. Informing is an art form. And you must learn it and practice it.

When you blow up and have unprocessed anger, you are a bear in a china house; it hurts everyone and everything around you. The Aura of a Manifestor is significant; it has IMPACT, it feels explosive to others. Part of your learning here is to understand the extent to which you impact the people around you so that you can tread more carefully.

You might also feel stuck, or like nothing you do yields fruit. So, after a lifetime of being trained to fit into a Generator world, usually by Generator teachers or parents, this process may have dulled your ability to go out there and make shizz happen. You may have been controlled or forced to wait for the others before running out to go manifest stuff. "Act more accordingly, or you will piss people off, slow down, or wait for the right thing to come along." These statements might be the gist of what you may have heard growing up. So, if you have not been manifesting the world you are inspired to live in, and you are feeling more anger than peace, something is quite OFF for you.

You must understand your Aura is repelling; it says, get out of my way I am about to manifest something. Many people are afraid of this intense impact and may have been put off by you, misjudged your power, or were simply uncomfortable by your energy. So, if you are sacrificing what you want because you care what others think of you, listen up, Manifestor... and LISTEN WELL (most Manifestors can't hear coaching, so this might be hard for you, but if you get one thing – listen to this following sentence). You are supersonic and have wicked manifestation skills that might just have imploded because of conditioning, but don't let that stop you now. YUP, if you are stuck in your life, you have sacrificed yourself for others. You have been unable to get coaching help because most Manifestors inherently don't want to listen to others. (This is not a bad thing either, you aren't necessarily designed to take a lot of coaching.) But if you are angry and you are not willing to know that you are sacrificing your heart's desire, you might just continue on your life with all that Manifestor MOJO power somewhat snuffed out and dulled. If you don't use it, you lose it. So, getting your manifestation juice back on track might just take a little come-to-Jesus straight talk. Ask yourself, where have you been sacrificing your heart's desires for others? Where have you been sacrificing yourself for what others think of you? Are you afraid to be or act as the LONE WOLF you were designed to be? Or where have you simply been sacrificing your well-being for the well-being of others, including your family or children? Let's get straight here. If you want to manifest, you have to realign to your power. If you are trying to please others, fit in, be liked, bend backward to keep up with the Jones, then welcome to the Manifestor world of implosion. Meaning you will get nowhere.

If you start now, you can begin to listen to your Inner Authority, get the idea of what to do, inform those around you, move forward with action, watch the red carpet roll out for you.

Now for those of you super successful Manifestors out there, who are making the big bucks and sitting on super powerfully successful lives and businesses who are angry... YUP, this is super important for you. Although you are good at manifesting, if you strive in greed like heavily driven fashion for the next thing and burn yourself out, you are missing your entire reason for existence. It is not hitting that more significant 7-figure mark. NOPE, you are here to know PEACE. So, if you are aligned with INFORMING and are empowered as a Manifestor, now pull back and learn the truth of who you are... you should be driven to reach PEACE, not just stuff.

So, for you as a Manifestor, here are the steps to your success Strategy:

1. Listen inside to get clarity on your Inner Authority on what you want to manifest. (We will learn Inner Authority next; each Manifestor will have a different Inner Authority.)
2. Inform those that you will impact with your actions. Informing takes practice and patience. You are telling

     people what you plan to do, not telling others what they should do! Super important key distinction here.

3.   Move forward on your manifestation.

4.   Let the red carpet be rolled out for you. Meaning, let people support you.

5.   You really cannot course correct your manifestation until after the process is complete. So, don't try and figure anything out in advance. You will only know after the fact if that action and manifestation brought PEACE.

6.   Delegate the bulk of the busy work. You are not meant to work full 8-hour workdays. Manage your energy and get Manifesting!

7.   Are you feeling peaceful or angry as shizz? If angry, do some healing work, slow down, and ask yourself, are you calm and relaxed or peaceful before initiating something? Are your Manifestations bringing you peace? Those energies should be a large part of your barometer on all actions.

8.   When you feel it is time to initiate, you should move forward with a sense of calm and peace, not out of fear or feeling frantic.

9.   If there has been wounding, pain from the past: then learning how to find a silent inner center will assist your process.

Manifestors, you are meant to be a nonconformist. Don't be afraid of what people think of you. Act in your power. You have the right to manifest a life you love. It doesn't mean losing all your scruples. You want to act in alignment with high values and the rest of your chart, of course.

So, you are here to know peace. If you are angry, you are in your Not-Self theme.

Manifestors, you must inform before acting. You must be willing to understand the impact you have on others. You will learn this over time by informing. If many people in your inner circle are acting out as rageaholics, consider how your behavior impacts those around you. Waiting happens for you before the idea comes; an idea will come based on your Inner Authority. Once you are clear on what to manifest, tell the world, then move forward, and the oceans will part, for it is time for you to manifest. Informing takes practice and patience. (I know you usually have little of this, but it is crucial.) Once you have started the ball rolling, then you will need to delegate the daily grind to other people. If you are burned out or exhausted, well, you will have no power left. All those memes about how tired Projectors are, well, that goes for you too. Overwork will drain you quickly, and you will have no force left for your true purpose.

Most of the world as we know it was created by Manifestors. They made things happen and told the rest of us how we should do something to manifest. "Just do it. Just go out there and grab destiny. Step out into the world and implement. Make the world see your vision and take it. You can make things happen." This kind of thinking was told to us by those who created this world, who stepped out and made things happen. However, for the rest of the population, if they employ these tactics, they suffer. They will get burned out, bitter, frustrated, they might have some success, but they will feel an overwhelming sense of discomfort. They might try and numb out this discomfort with opiates, drugs, wine, TV, etc.

So, let's not all try to live like Manifestors. OK? They are only 9% of the population. Even though we are all conditioned to live as Manifestors, it is only correct for this small portion of the population to INITIATE ACTION.

Let that settle in for a moment.

No wonder we have a world full of furious and confused, people.

Manifestors
Strategy: To Inform
Signature: Peace
Not-Self Theme: Anger
Your Aura: It is impactful and moves forward with gusto, moving smaller Auras out of the way. Usually, this is uncomfortable for other people to get knocked around. Think someone jumping into the pool cannonball style while casual swimmers are floating on the swan rafts sipping Mai Tais; they are not too happy about the splashing and the waves. So, you are here to learn and understand how intense this is for people. Not to make yourself small, but to Inform all of those people nicely (again, do not tell people what to do), just inform them what you are going to do so that people can move out of the way, cover their drinks and prepare for the splash.

2. Generators and Manifesting Generators

So many of you are either Generators or Manifesting Generators, and for you, you must employ a very, very, very different tactic in life than all the other Types.

YOU READY? Let's GO!

When I refer to GENERATORS in the terms of your initial STRATEGY, it will be the same starting point for MANIFESTING GENERATORS, so let's get into it! (Manifesting Generators, you are unique to yourselves; I have more on this in the accompanying PDF, but you must understand and begin with this basic Strategy too!) The Aura Strategy for both Manifesting Generators and Generators is the same. However, after this initial Strategy, several things make the Manifesting Generator very unique.

For you Generators/MGs, you must learn TO WAIT (FIRST) then TO RESPOND.

Wait, before you act, wait before you initiate, wait before you take any kind of action. WHAT? Not just make it happen? Wait?

Now, what coach or self-help guru is going to tell you to wait? Not too many. So, think of yourself as lucky. A tiny percentage of the population is getting this information and will be willing to experiment with it. Yet, just this small piece of intel alone can shift your entire life from one of massive chaos and extreme frustration to aligning with work you love in a fully satisfied, juicy way!

So Generators and Manifesting Generators... "Wait To Respond" is your new success code mantra. What this means is your Aura is magnetic; it is drawing things in towards you. Your Aura is warm fuzzy energy; people love this Aura. And you are here to bring in the people, circumstances, the right programs, books you are meant to attract in towards you. You are pulling this energy into you like a magnetic force field. When you initiate or try to go out there and make something happen, you push things away; you work so hard, then you burn out and get super frustrated.

So, for you, when you wait, you must watch what is showing up around you. You are on the right track if you draw in a "sign" or a "synchronicity" after contemplating a new idea or action to take. You might think, "Hey, it is time for me to start an online business." Instead of leaping out there and spending 5k-100k on the next course (if you have just gone out and purchased that new high-end coaching program, relax, we have all made that mistake before), just wait, watch for signs, outside confirmations first. Once you get that confirmation, then move forward. Honestly, I know I am biased, but the results would quadruple if everyone just did our Human Design certification courses before investing in any coaching, therapy, or anything dealing with clients. It is very challenging to know what coaching tools will work properly until you know your Design.

Generators and Manifesting Generators, your energy is like the golden goose, a commodity for the world. It drives, lights up, creates, works, and moves things. It is very much needed in this world. However, this energy has been used and controlled without anyone acknowledging that this energy is very valuable. In other words, giant corporations (this is just one example) may work people to the bone without really honoring the energy force or creativity most of the workers bring without letting them respond, or making sure they are fulfilled and satisfied just using their energy as a human battery. (OMG, *The Matrix* was REAL.)

But, here is the deal. YOU HAVE THE POWER to CHOOSE TO RESPOND. Yes, it is essential for you to know that you do not have to give your energy over to anything or anyone or any company that is NOT correct for you. When you align to things that feel satisfying and on fire, you serve the world. If you are doing work you hate that frustrates you or makes you feel shitty, you are handing over a sacred commodity for the sake of money, comfort, or whatever the reason may be.

You are here to do the work you love. A Generator on fire is waking up aligned, super excited about the day, doing cartwheels to your next task. You are here to be wholly aligned with your daily activities, to-do list, and how you make money. You should be excited to get up in the morning, super excited to do everything you do, exhaust all your energy, and sort of collapse at the end of the day onto the bed exhausted. If you don't exercise or use up all that energy, you might run all sorts of unused energy around in your head that keep you up all night. Not fun for a Projector in the house who is absorbing all that toxic stew.

You are the creative, brilliant commodity on the planet that, if you are aligned, you should, instead, wake up in the middle of the night driven by inspiration and be unable to contain yourself; you are so excited!

So if you are feeling down, frustrated, burned out, angry or unhappy with your work, let your ears perk up because you are living as your Not-Self. And this is not good for anyone!

So, the process goes like this for Generators and Manifesting Generators:

1. Your Aura is bringing you what you want! (So, just chill, beauty, your Aura has this.)
2. You have a million ideas (but don't act on any). I know, I know this is super stressful, especially for my MGs out there that have a lot of energy, but if you can trust, this will save you so much angst.
3. You wait for an OUTSIDE (**NOT** an inner download or inner knowing) – it must be an OUTSIDE – confirmation from a friend, a billboard, magazine, TV, radio, or any outside source confirming your idea. Think of a sign or synchronicity to the multitude of ideas you are thinking of acting on.
4. Once you get this confirmation, then check your inner authority. (Find out more on your Inner Authority next.)
5. You get the GO from confirmation, and you are checking in with your Inner Authority – then take action forward. WOO-HOO, it's then super sexy go mode!
6. Check how satisfied you feel while acting.
7. Are you feeling satisfied doing the activity? Are you satisfied after the fact? Do you love this job, or do you love the activities you are doing? If so, voila, then you are on the right track! And you will start to feel satisfied and supersonic all the time!
8. If you feel frustrated, exhausted, or burned-out in the work you are doing/life you're living, start looking for something to respond to, TO GET OUT NOW (I know this is far easier said than done)! Because you are wasting your precious commodity, your life force energy!

The Generator energy carries with it the powerful life force of the planet. Here we see love, sex, power, procreation, business, work, and sustainable energy. The Defined Sacral is truly the life force, energy, commodity, fuel for humanity. The most important aspect of this Defined Sacral is to know that your energy is a sanctified, valuable, a wanted commodity. It should be considered sacred. If you give your energy over to anything that you are not satisfied doing, quite simply, you will suffer. If you listen to the conditioning from: your mind, your teachers, parents, schools, bosses, that tell you that YOU SHOULD take a specific action, but you just HATE DOING IT. If you continue in this direction, your life will feel like an energy suck all the time. It will be like a mighty black cloud force of ongoing frustration. You might just feel like a vast 4-wheeler truck stuck in the sand. You have a lot of power, you are working so hard each day, but after long hours of grinding, you have only moved four feet, and you might just feel BURNED OUT! The good news, it doesn't take a Generator long to replenish themselves, but it is tough to awaken your life purpose when you are burned out. Most of humanity is burned out, conditioned to work, to push, to initiate action, and to move, move, move, engage in busy work and never check in with what exactly is suitable for the individual.

As a Defined Sacral, you are here to respond to life, not initiate action. When you learn this sacred superpower (TO RESPOND), you will find that life runs more smoothly and awakens you to a world of ease and grace, and extreme satisfaction. First, you must overcome the fears, the mind, and the conditioning. You must learn your Inner Authority and practice living your experiment. When you align with the proper way to use the Sacral energy, this 4-wheeler turbo Mack Truck will be up and running over hills, up San Francisco streets, jumping over bumps cruising at high speed. When you do work you love and are on purpose, you will leap out of bed with enthusiasm. You will be able to work, exercise often, have a day filled with lots of to-dos, go to bed exhausted, and still wake up refreshed, renewed, and inspired, ready for more. Without Responding, you might just have a day filled with busy to-dos, no real purpose, and a whole lot of unfulfilled frustration running around. Just look out at most of humanity, and you will know what I am talking about. The let's just get it done, move faster, go to the next task, run another errand, coffee to wake up, wine to go to bed, no slowing down, no waiting, just frenetic movement in no real direction. Part of your life purpose is finding work that makes you feel satisfied inside and out, and aligns with your deepest values and the rest of your chart. This work, when on point, can be profoundly gratifying and satisfying for you. A life running around frantically frustrated all day or a juicy, delicious, satisfying good to the last drop type of life – you choose.

Generators and Manifesting Generators
Strategy: Wait to Respond
Signature: Satisfaction
Not-Self Theme: Frustration
Your Aura: Your Aura is comforting for people; it is magnetic. It draws in people, life circumstances, opportunities when you allow it to. When you learn to wait, all of these magical things can come your way. When you act after response, you will feel a glow of satisfaction that will bring much-needed ease to your work and personal life.

3. Projectors

For all my lovely Projectors, listen up! You most definitely suffer the most in this day and age compared to every other Auric Type. I can say that because, as you know by now, I too am a Projector. We are here to be like the wise women/men up outside the mainstream, the archetype of the wise man on the hill. People come from miles around to seek our sage wisdom and advice. We have visions, insights, ideas, advice for people in high volume. When we are revered and sought, recognized

– oh wow, can people learn a lot from us, and they will come from miles away just to listen to our sage advice. They don't steal our visions from us or claim them to be theirs; they honor and acknowledge the genius as support for them. Excuse me for one moment as I choke on the irony. Because we, as a society, are just not quite there yet.

Here is the problem in the modern world. You just don't get paid for sitting up on a hill studying and learning and mastering things, especially when no one recognizes your wisdom as of yet. And no one respects those people who appear lazy, talking, sitting upon a hill all day, acting like they know it all. You see, Projectors, our time has not yet come. The majority of the population just does not get us yet. So chances are it is either super lonely up on that hill, or you are shouting so loud and so hard for recognition with no one coming, you are hoarse, burned out, and well, just a wee bit bitter.

Partly why it is such an important calling for me to get this information out to the tribe! Because our time is coming, and we are here to lead this transmutation of human evolution. No pressure!

It is a bitter pill for the Generator world to swallow, and I don't know if they will take this well. Yup, guess what, Generators: the workforce is meant to be led, conducted, directed, and advised by people who can only work 2-3 maybe 4 hours a day. Then rest, relax, play, and do nothing. Everyone just take a breath in with me here; it's OK, we will survive this. I worked in the corporate world; I know this idea will give the CEOs a good shake in their boots.

If only the Projectors could trust their value and their unique design. So they could sit back and let the Universe arrange a career that doesn't drain them of everything they have. However, most Projectors have been caught up in the Generator energy, absorbing, distorting, and amplifying it, trying so hard to keep up, compete with the rat race, hold steady in the hustle

9-hour workforce that they just have no self-esteem left. They have often been beaten down for so long, it is hard to recover.

A Projector living the Not-Self theme is most likely running around like a chicken with its head cut off, thinking it is a Manifesting Generator. They are absorbing and amplifying the world's population of Generators and acting like they are super Generators, never knowing when enough is enough. You might see a Projector in extreme burnout, adrenal fatigue, chronic pain, extremely bitter; they just see that life appears to be easier for everyone else, and it just plain sucks for them. Also, their Aura is like a straw sucking in all the toxicity soup of the world, and it can be very excruciating for Projectors. So those Projectors in a toxic environment have less of a shield against the damage it can do.

They might have issues with addiction, food, sex, drugs to the extreme level. So take heed, fellow Projectors, and please hear me; it's going to be OK now!

You are here to lead, guide, direct, and ask questions. You are here to live as an example to the Generators to work smarter, not harder, and definitely NOT LONGER, and share with them that they are not here to be slaves or cogs in the system. Because quite frankly, they can do it much longer than Projectors, but they will burn out too. They will learn from Projectors that they no longer have to use their Generator fuel as slaves any longer. Projectors will burn out much faster and might even drop dead first if they don't get out, but Generators will fry their circuits as well if they aren't living in their correct line of work.

So, what do you do, poor Projector?

Unplug first off from as much Generator fuel as possible. You might need to work in your own office, sleep in your own bed, go take naps in the car at lunch. Or, if it is possible in your life, try to live a simplified lifestyle away from the busy everyday hustle and grind. Try to manage your energy with extreme health, including green juice, superfoods, and high vibe meditation, chants, mantras, whatever you can do to lift your energy up. Live by your joy and master systems.

Get quiet, and DO NOT, I repeat, DO NOT give anyone unsolicited advice, insight, or information. WAIT until they ask for it. Sit back and wait to see who asks you questions, what they are asking you about, and then provide them with your genuine golden insight. Do not cast your pearls before swine, as they say. If you don't have any treasures of wisdom, go get some! Your life will be so much easier if you can CHARGE premium prices for a consultant rate that gets you in and out on your schedule. You must be a master of a system to be seen. Whatever you do, do not try to be seen or try to be noticed. When you do, you will either be in excruciating pain, or have your ideas stolen, or you just might simply be ignored. Or worse yet, and this happens often, you speak your ideas, wisdom, knowledge, and people don't listen to you; they just claim it as their own. It is the story of my life.

Because most Projectors are not recognized, this drives many to act out in extreme ways to be heard. They talk louder, even scream (people who know me are seriously rolling on the floor laughing out loud right now), push to be the star or center of attention. They are desperate to be heard, for a good reason too. Projectors are here to be recognized and live IN SUCCESS! The bad news, you can't push it or make it happen; it has to come to you. However, how the heck were you supposed to know this? LOL. Relief. You are getting it now. So take a breath in with me; the worst is over.

Important note for Projectors. Many people seem to think that Human Design is an opportunity for Projectors just to revel in laziness. So, hold on a moment; I am climbing up on my soapbox. Do not let the Generator world intimidate you. First, honor your own genius, shimmering beauty, and unique being, then celebrate other Projectors. Most Manifesting Generators/ Generators (I am leaving Reflectors out of this), and Manifestors do not know what it is like being a Projector, most of whom are trying to guide and teach this intel when it is the Projector who should be coaching and leading. But because we have trouble keeping up and rising to the top of the entrepreneurial pyramid in the seven-figure income bracket, people tend to look to other Types as leaders. Also, if a Manifestor is trying to knock you down and bulldoze your genius, ask them nicely to step to the F-back. It is the Projector that needs to be recognized finally, and it might start with Projectors recognizing each other because the rest of the world just does not get it yet. So please, do the entire world a favor and go out there and route for a Projector! If you are a Manifestor, Generator or MG, and you are throwing up your hands, saying to yourself, "Go, Projectors," and giving a little booty twerk, there is an exceptional place in heaven for you! (And in my heart.) Because we all know, Projectors are a little slow, they may be struggling, they might not be hitting the million-dollar mark yet (obviously there are plenty of Projectors that have, but the majority suffer first), but they have golden insights dipped in diamonds, and if you just let them speak these gems, their wisdom might just change the world, and they friggin need to be heard! Sorry, someone had to say it!

Lastly, as you Decondition and seriously try this on, learn to WAIT FOR THE INVITATION, WAIT TO BE RECOGNIZED. Your Auric field will demand people to invite you! It will happen, so rest assured you will get seen for your genius, you will be invited, and YOU WILL LIVE A LIFE OF SUCCESS! If you can follow this Strategy, it is what you are designed for.

So, the process goes like this for Projectors:

1.   Wait to be Invited – Your Aura is demanding for those WHO NEED YOUR WISDOM to invite you to speak, lead, or provide guidance (so, relax, gorgeous one, your Aura has this).

2.   You have a million things to say to people; you have

advice, clarity, and so much knowledge on how people can do something more straightforward (but you don't speak on any of this). I know it is excruciating. When you are asked, then you can share your diamond shade of higher knowledge the world is longing for! But ONLY THEN!

3. If you don't have any insight, you must learn to master a system. Projectors are judged far more harshly when you speak on topics. So make sure you master your methods before sharing your insights.

4. Stay quiet and watch. People will start asking you questions. What do they want to know from you? Where are they inviting you?

5. Once you get this invitation, you must then check your particular Inner Authority. (We are going into this in the next chapter.) We all have different Inner Authorities to use before we accept an invitation.

6. Listen to the Inner Authority. If this is the proper invitation, then take action forward. WOO-HOO, it's now a much smoother ride! You will have the energy for action once you are invited and recognized. Like magic, it will be so much easier! No more Mr./Mrs. Bitter.

7. Feel into the JOY as a guide. Are you feeling successful and having fun? Then you know, you are living the proper invitation. No, it doesn't have to be a hand-written engraved invitation. Often it comes in the form of recognition or simply a question.

8. Are you feeling bitter? Do you feel anxious or overworked with what you are doing? If so, you are not advising the right group. So, wait for the following invitation, then move on.

9. Are you over-giving wanting people to hear you, so you give free sessions, free advice, and then getting bitter? This never works.

10. If you feel joyous, energized, inspired, you are making the right money and only working when you have the energy – you are on the right track!

11. If you listen to people tell you how to succeed, and you just start initiating action to reach a goal, you will most likely get burned out and bitter. Or worse – I have many Projector clients who come to me after years of living like this, from the motivational, self-help, high-end coaching world, and they are ill, have chronic diseases, or are unable to get off the couch.

So, for Projectors, rest assured, you are not lazy, you do not need to keep up, you do not need to fight for your ideas, you can relax. When you sit back, watch, wait, master your system, pay close attention to your energy field. Things will get so much easier for you, and your life will begin to turn on, become successful, and simplify.

Projectors
Strategy: Wait For the Invitation (Recognition)
Signature: Success
Not-Self Theme: Bitterness
Aura: Your Aura penetrates the other like a laser, and your Aura also absorbs the energy around it, and then it jets out like a knife cutting into the Aura of the other. So, you can imagine how uncomfortable this is for the other people around you. If you are uninvited, it is painful for those people you are lasering with your advice. The Invitation is to protect you and them, to the right people who feel inspired, alive, awakened by your genius. Once this minor fix happens, you will feel on purpose, all doors will open, and the bitterness will fade. Yes, it takes a Projector a little longer, but you will get there. You will be completely different when you arrive!

4. Reflectors

Reflectors, you need to know you are the very rare Type in this system; you have a vital role to play for all of humanity. You are like the temperature for us all. Are we aligned and healthy or not?

Look back on your life and your environments. Checking if you are in the right place based on the health of the situation is a key for you. Look back on your life and ask the questions: Are there times you felt good? Are there times you knew your location was toxic? Were there times in your life you knew you were in the right place, and it was super healthy for you? Look at your life currently and ask yourself, do you feel great in your job, home or relationship? Are there times you feel, sense, or taste that something is wrong for you? Do you know when it is time to leave an unhealthy environment? Are you willing to move to a healthy place, relationship, or career? Contemplate.

Consider, as Ra Uru Hu said, if all 1% of the Reflectors of the world were in the right location, we could heal the planet and all of humanity. I'm paraphrasing, but something to this degree.

Why do people stay in environments that aren't healthy, you ask? Great question!

Usually, people's minds are conditioned to believe that they cannot move on, or they have to stay for the good of the family or to pay the bills. They talk themselves out of leaving. But you can, and you absolutely SHOULD, and continue until you find the perfect spot.

So, in this system, the Reflector is the unicorn. The Reflectors are unique, have a unique way of operating, and should be treated as such. The Reflectors will have a magical ability to report back what is happening in the environment; they taste it. They sample the energies around them and, like a fine wine connoisseur with the most sophisticated pallet, they can give a detailed report of every delicious flavor, color, variation, nuance, age, creative analogies of the aroma of each glass. If you have a Reflector in your life, child, family member, coworker, or member of your community in any way, shape, or form, pay close attention. This BEING is like having a giant mirror up in the house, office, group, or community. If you listen, they will taste, sample, and reflect back on the health of the environment they are involved with. If they are depressed, withdrawn, or focusing on materialism or things that annoy you, chances are they are reflecting YOU and the environment you are in. Reflectors are, yup, you guessed it, vast reflections of the environment they are in. You will definitely see it in the Reflector children. If they are unhealthy, the atmosphere is unhealthy, just that simple. If they don't want to be somewhere, they should be allowed to say no. The conditioning for a Reflector is so purely 100%; there is just no avoiding it. They absorb the whole environment and reflect it back. Think of the moon; it has no light of its own, it is just reflecting the sun. So, how we deal with Reflectors in our lives is to honor them as unique, give them time, and never pressure them to rush, get things done, hurry up, or force a decision – absolutely challenging in the modern world. Many Reflectors have trouble just being a part of the homogenized world. But, particularly if you have a Reflector child. The Generator world as a whole is pushing with speed: get to school, your next class, get your homework done, do this program, that program, etc. Get up early, get to work, rush to the gym, get to the store, move faster, and quick decisions are honored. So understanding how to support a Reflector in the practical world is something we all, as a humanity, need to contemplate. If you are a Reflector, do not let anyone or anything rush you. You will need time for decisions, a lot of it. Consider waiting for the entire moon cycle feeling out how you are experiencing the choice in each stage of the cycle. If you get good at tracking the cycle, you will notice repeating themes through your Gates month after month. This type of journaling will help you understand how the transits move through your chart.

So, the progress goes like this for a Reflector:

1. You need to honor your uniqueness first!
2. Pay attention to your environment and how it makes you feel. Do you have a unique chair, place in the house you love? Or do you need to leave your environment altogether?
3. How do you feel when you enter a car? Is there discomfort anywhere you spend a lot of time?
4. Are you happy in the job, career, or place where you spend most of your time? If not, are you willing to leave?
5. You are here to wait for a full 28-day lunar cycle before making a decision. I KNOW IT SOUNDS CRAZY. So, here is the thing when you are up against a powerful decision, do not let anyone pressure your YES OR NO. You are allowed to take your time.
6. Wait an entire 28-30 days before letting anyone know whether you are a yes or no. Do not make any decision during that time. Just feel into the potential, and you should get clear after a complete lunar cycle.
7. There are ways to understand how the star weather or transits move through your chart each day. They will create a cycle of Channels that become defined based on your hanging Gates. You can learn about this technique and chart it out based on your Gates, and I believe this is super useful for many Reflectors. It can be a little complicated and not something I will outline here. So, my best advice is to SLOW DOWN ~ Find the best possible location for everything you do! Where you live, sleep, and sit through the day, even your car. And wait before making any significant decision. That alone is going to serve you GREATLY!!
8. Lastly, look for those people who want to know what you have to say and what you are reflecting. You want to be around people that make you feel good!

Reflectors
Strategy: Wait for a full Lunar Cycle before making a decision
Signature: Awe or the wonderment of life
Not-Self Theme: Disappointment
Your Aura: Your Aura tastes and samples the environment. You are here to give a full read on the places you are living, working, visiting. Allow yourself to explore those environments you love, pay attention to people who allow you to shine and reflect, share your experience. Are you healthy? Is there anything you need to do to feel more alive? You are essential; let your Unicorn rainbow colors be seen in the world!

Exercise for Each Type
Now it is time to experiment: Look back on your past and ask yourself a couple of questions to confirm if any of this stuff might have some truth for you.

1. When you did things in your past that turned out to be horribly uncomfortable, did you inadvertently enter the situation against your Design? In other words, did you go against your Strategy? Did you push, shove, or initiate? Or for Manifestors, did you wait too long or care what others thought?

2. When in your past were you aligned and full of life? Did you initiate? Did you respond? Were you invited? Did you wait before jumping in? Did this result in a better experience for you? Check in for **your TYPE** – and compare with your past. It is beneficial to observe your history to notice times when you may have been properly in your Strategy without knowing it, and yet that was when everything magically worked out for you. You may not have understood why some things worked out miraculously for you while other times you suffered. So, now you can contemplate this, and perhaps it will shed some insight for you.

3. Do an overview of your life right now and your past. Contemplate, does any of this resonate with you? Look at the Not-Self theme (just for your Type), which comes when you go against your Strategy and contemplate if you have ever felt this way before. Write out the times you have felt your Signature Theme and your Not-Self Theme. Do you notice patterns?

4. You can contemplate this in terms of relationships, businesses, career choices, any other major decisions like moving or going to school, etc.

Take the time to contemplate, spend time journaling, reviewing your past. Take as much time as you need here. A little contemplation can be a magical experience. Contemplation is just a gentle way to explore your past actions and notice any AHA moments that may come forward for you. Contemplative discoveries may help inform your journey of Deconditioning and assist you in the experiment moving forward.

My experiences living as a Splenic Projector who was conditioned to believe she was a Manifesting Generator. First off, I was a competitive gymnast at eight years old, working out five hours a day, six days a week. Most Projectors are not natural athletes; those who are might just find themselves injured more than everyone else. Let us just say, I pretty much grew up in a hospital. Then in my 20s, as I mentioned, I pushed and shoved with all my might to manifest my dream of being a professional choreographer. I created an entire performance group unrecognized as the leader; the whole troop was stolen from under me. I took a full year off, pretty much passed out on the couch to decompress from the adventure. Managed to get a high-end over 6-figure corporate salary working from home. The other coworkers worked an average of 12-hour days; I worked three (telling no one as I slept most days till noon). Still managing to outperform the team. This career did stem from recognition and was quite fulfilling. I was very good at it, climbed quite high up the ladder.

In general, though, I have had sore throats most days trying to be heard. I tried everything to be seen, recognized, and believed. My spiritual prowess was mocked, belittled, unrecognized, and made fun of most of the time. I would try and share my shamanic journeys with people, but I was inevitably scorned, scoffed at, or dismissed. Most definitely this made me doubt that I had anything important to say before discovering my Human Design. I have the Shamanic Channel, designed to be a heretic. WOW, this assisted me in honoring my wisdom, keeping my mouth shut but valuing my gifts. So, I hope you can see some aspects in your past as well.

What has your experience been? Have you noticed when you pushed to make something happen, you ended up in a cluster-f-ck? Have you been burned-out or beaten down trying things your coaches tell you to do only to end up with mud on the face?

As a Generator, ask yourself if when you take action towards a goal without checking for outside confirmations, do you feel frustrated? Do you notice when you do work you love, your energy skyrockets? If you do things you hate, do you feel drained and burned out or depleted? Are you using all your energy before you go to bed with exercise, or do you lay in bed face up, unable to sleep? Are you fulfilled in your career?

Manifestors, are you friggin angry? Do people get you? Are you taking action or waiting for people to allow you to do what you want? Do you need approval? Do you notice that when you are feeling confident, you have moments where things manifest like magic?

Reflectors, have you noticed a sick feeling when entering into a room, car, or building? Are you able to be yourself and let people think you are weird? Or are you trying to fit into a world, lifestyle, or experience that is not right for you?

Take the time to write down your experiences with your Type before we move on.

Chapter 7

Insomnia Much? How You Are Designed to Sleep

Sleep is the Swiss army knife of health. When sleep is deficient, there is sickness and disease. And when sleep is abundant, there is vitality and health.
Matthew Walker

We all know the power of sleep, yet so many people suffer in this area. Do you have any issues sleeping? Well, each Type is designed to sleep a little differently, so learning a few tips and tricks might completely cure your insomnia issues. I have had many clients who have problems with sleep, and these little tips completely transformed their lives. I will give you a couple of basic steps on this.

The first thing you learn in Human Design is that you should sleep alone, all Types. I know, I know; it feels shocking. It goes against everything we have ever been taught about the husband and wife, wife and wife, husband and husband, or whatever type of partnership you choose. One thing we all know, that we are told in this society today, is that you should share the same bed with your partner.

According to this knowledge, wherever you are Undefined, you are susceptible to the conditioning of those with that definition. They aren't doing anything wrong; there is no problem. It is just happening. So, if you can actively separate yourself from your partner while you sleep, you provide yourself time to Decondition. TO BE YOURSELF in your own Aura.

This experiment, of course, does not mean you can't have sex, and it does not mean you can't cuddle or watch TV together or have breakfast in bed.

It means for the eight hours you sleep, have two separate rooms with two separate beds. And... you're welcome!

At least for me, having my own queen-sized bed was something I have always loved. No one snoring (no offense, Davidian, LOL), I can wake up and start writing on my laptop at any hour, and I can stretch out, have the sheets I love and the mattress right for my body. Because my partner Davidian is as obsessed with Human Design as I am, we both acknowledge this has absolutely nothing to do with our intimacy, how close we are, our profound love and joy of being together, or anything. It is just part of the experiment.

Now, as a Projector, you should go to bed before you are tired. It would help if you had a good couple of hours to read, relax, unwind before falling asleep. There are NO ABSOLUTES in Human Design; we are all unique. So, a quick caveat if you know your advanced chart. There is an area called Determination; it has to do with the Design Sun and Earth. If you have Color Six and you have a right-facing arrow or are passive, then this means you are Indirect. (Check the PDF for more info on this.) These beings, even for Projectors, are considered Nocturnal. This is because they are connected to light. The Indirect are designed to stay up all night and sleep during the day. The Direct Color 6 people are the exact opposite. They are designed to be up with the sun and sleep when the sun goes down. All food and intel will digest better with this bit of adjustment. If you have no idea what in the world I am going on about right now, do not worry about it at all. I usually suggest people explore the basics for a good year, some people say at least seven years before learning this advanced aspect of your chart. This is just a little note for some people who can't sleep. It might be any Type, but no other Type is told to go to bed early. If you want to learn more about your Advanced chart, check out the PDF in the bonus materials at: https://foxy5d.com/pages/are-you-a-mutant.

The Generators are designed to not go to bed until you

drop. Sounds crazy. But if you are living correctly, you should be super excited to get up in the morning, do what you love, respond, align, love your work, do your exercise, and then crash out at night. If you can't sleep, it just might be you did not wholly release your Generator fuel and/or you haven't had enough exercise for the day. So, go out there and get out there and rock out your beautiful, brilliant Generator fuel doing shizz you love. Once you wake up, you will feel bright-eyed, and bushy-tailed, and ready for action. Your energy should be restored. If you feel drained or like you have no desire at all to do the work you are in, it might be a sign to start over with waiting to respond to something new.

Manifesting Generators, this is similar for you. However, once you go to bed, you can read, work, or take care of a few things while letting the rest of the Generator fuel fall off from the system and then let yourself fall asleep. You will probably wake up rested, restored, and with regenerative energy for another fantastic creative, vibrant day like the Generator.

Manifestors – Like the other Undefined Sacrals, the Projectors, and Reflectors, you will need more sleep than the Generators. You might like a midday nap or simply go to bed before being tired and let yourself fall asleep when tired after a few hours of bed unwinding, like reading or listening to a podcast. But, sleeping alone might be a beneficial tip for finding your unique energy, so you don't overtax your system. Living with Generators can be complex on a Manifestor. No one is here to tell a Manifestor what to do, so this is just a suggestion to experiment with and see if this works for you.

Reflectors – This will be similar to the other Undefined Sacral beings, the Projector and the Manifestor. You must try to go to bed early before you are tired. However, also for a Reflector, you must feel good in the sacred sleep space. Spend time doing your favorite in-bed activity, reading, watching a movie, listening to Audible (that is mine). Your environment is so crucial for you. So, make sure you love your bed, your sheets, the entire sleep ritual, and if you can sleep alone, it will really help your connection with your moon and in order to Decondition.

Sleeping is such a significant part of life; when we sleep well, we live well! It is also an incredibly crucial role in the process of Deconditioning and becoming who you are designed to be. Your unique magical, beautiful self. If this is an issue with the person you love, be sure and let them know a couple of super essential points:

- You still love them dearly.
- You still want to cuddle and be close.
- This will not affect your relationship.
- This will not affect your intimacy or sex-life.
- Think of it as a fun experiment and journey to better sleep and dreams.
- Have fun making your bed precisely as you like it!

Remember sleeping terms are a homogenized societal imprint and shouldn't dictate how we sleep.

Alright, everyone, sweet dreams, and enjoy your favorite pillow all to yourself. PS. One of the things I love about gratitude is seeing the beauty in the little things. So, loving your sheets, your pillows is a beautiful way to shift out of any stress, center at the moment, honor your life, and ease into dreams. See our PDF for some of our favorite magical pillows.

Chapter 8

Inner Authority – Your Personalized GPS System

Choices are the hinges of destiny.
Pythagoras

I told you I was going to help install your very own personalized GPS system to take you to a life you love. Well, hold on, this is essential stuff, so pull out your journals. Making a decision can often feel like a very intense thing to do in life. Often, we look back at those significant crossroads and think, what if I chose something else? I have quite a few of those moments. One, in particular, was turning down a scholarship to NYU for an MFA degree. I didn't regret it until my creative venture went sideways, and I had to reevaluate my life. I wondered, what would have happened if I had just taken that direction in life? I had a lot of regret about that decision for a good couple of years. Primarily because I began to realize that I didn't make this decision on my own. I was super influenced by people around me telling me their opinions about college, books I was reading on making a decision at the time. Of course, I had no cohesive natural way of knowing which direction I should take in my life based on my uniqueness. It wasn't until I finally found my way to my proper life and career calling that I stopped regretting that choice. The point is that it is hard to know if we made the right life decisions, particularly on big life-changing choices.

There are many different teachings around decision-making. Many of my clients have learned endless spiritual techniques around how to choose the right paths. Some of these include following your intuition, making lists, going to psychics, using pendulums, getting downloads, following your heart, doing what you love, listening to your guides, using tarot cards, or spiritual channeling. All of these things are excellent tools, and yet, even after knowing all of these things, including therapy and years of deep processing work – I would still make one wrong decision after another. So do most people!

Why and how? I wondered, why did I make that choice, why did that turn out so badly?

In Human Design, we understand this. We get noticeably clear on why people are making choices based on conditioning and how to unearth this process so you can finally choose based on your unique self. So, according to Human Design, you are the master and complete sovereign of your decision-making. Feel into this for a moment; it is both empowering and overwhelmingly scary. So, all those gurus, tarot readers, even self-help coaches telling you what to do are going to lose a job as a back seat driver in your life. ALL OF THE POWER is now being taken back from the hands of anyone out there – it is being brought back into your own personal empowered decision-making process.

Here is what is super interesting about this, we are all designed to make decisions differently! If you think about this, it is pretty radical. We are told that there are many ways to make decisions, yet no one can understand why one of these ways may work for some people and not for others. It is never explained that each one of us should make decisions differently, and it should be based on your unique Inner Authority and nothing else. No, not unless you are studying this stuff, will you learn this incredible life-altering little nugget of gold. And another radical point to this is each decision-making process is very, very different. One Type is slow and needs time. Yup, those sales techniques that say you only have 24 hours and the pressure quotes that claim you are CEO-level leadership if you can make quick and final decisions: absolutely INCORRECT for 50% of the population. Some of us are super quick, and others need to talk it out. Still, others need to wait an excruciatingly long period over a whole month before ever moving forward on a life-changing decision. Again, I ask you to pause on this. If this is true, and you will never know for sure unless you try, think about the impact it could have. If this is true, which it is for every one of my clients, think about the POWER IN THIS. A key no one is talking about, to give you the ability to choose life-altering decisions in the right way every time. A technique that will provide every person confidence in that what they choose for themself will work out for the greatest good, lead them to a path they were born for, careers they love, life on purpose, and assist them in selecting the right relationships. This is friggin huge. WHY or why aren't more people shouting about this little technique that could change everyone's life in game-changing ways? Well, don't just sit there; go out and share this book with the world (if it is correct for you based on your IA, of course). I'm joking but serious as well. Knowing IA has radically changed my life, and so many people in our community and others who love this intel will attest it is beyond revolutionary.

So, making a list with pros and cons is not suitable for any Type; overthinking, analyzing, and letting the mind tell you what to do is also not correct for anyone either. Talk about a complete 180 in how to operate; this tool could potentially change your life.

Suppose you have been trained like most of us to use a decision-making process entirely opposite of what is correct for you. In that case, this might be the reason you have been suffering, or at the very least, have found yourself in uncomfortable situations.

NO! Not because you are low vibe, not because you are inherently flawed, or sabotaging yourself, not because you are misaligned, but because you are not using a correct decision-making process for your uniqueness. Let that settle in for a moment.

Now consider this. If I said, here is your magic GPS system – it is going to take you to a life you love. A life where you get to play out the unique puzzle piece of who you are precisely and be compensated handsomely for it. You don't have to pretend anymore! You don't have to be someone you are not. You don't have to live a life that you don't love. You don't have to work in a job that doesn't recognize you, burns you out, or that you don't 100% LOVE with all your heart. You just need to follow this magic GPS SYSTEM, and you will be led to the perfect decision every time. Here is the caveat: I know, I know, yes, there is another caveat. This GPS system is not your mind! And your mind will probably give you all kinds of reasons why you should not follow it. It will tell you this stuff is nuts. This girl, Raquel, is just a woo-woo wippy woo and will tell you a million explanations why you should not follow your inner GPS system. Why would your mind do that? Why would your mind lead you astray to a life you hate? How could your mind be so aggressively moving you against your own true path?

Let me give you an example of how this might play out if someone is trying to decide whether to take a job or not. This is how it might unfold. See, Human Design is not a belief system. You can't just agree or disagree with me; it will do you no good. You will have to experiment with this stuff to see if it works for you or not. If not, and your life is smooth, and you always make great decisions, then fine, just ignore this. If you are frustrated, burned out, bitter, feeling like you deserve a better life, angry about something, disappointed by the world, or plain and simply you are just tired of the way things are going – then you will want to try this out for yourself. So, back to my example, you have to decide to take this job or not. The job looks good on paper. Basically, you get a job offer in your ideal location, paying 100k more than your last job, you get a company car, and your office overlooks the ocean. However, your decision-making GPS SAYS NO! Your mind says, but this is an ideal job, you are not in a position to turn this down, you need this job, you have to start making money now, it is the perfect opportunity. Etc., etc. This is where the rubber then hits the proverbial road. Will you take the path of the magic GPS directing you, or will you let the MIND win? Often if you wait for the right direction and your Inner GPS says now this is the RIGHT job, a couple of weeks later, and it is higher-paying and in a better location, then it all makes sense. However, sometimes you just don't know why the GPS system says no, and you may never know why! So, you may get the NO on visiting friends who have made dinner plans and disrupt the whole evening for everyone. You don't understand why it is a NO, you may not ever find out. Maybe if you ate at that restaurant, you would have run into an ex, eaten a lousy piece of meat, or choked, or who knows, but that is the tricky part. The mind might not ever get its crazy need to know everything answered.

And this, my beautiful friend, who is on the journey with me now, and I honor you for this, is the choice you will continuously have to make. Trust the Inner Authority or let the crazy mind continue to go berserk; now that is the million-dollar question.

As you learn your unique GPS system and how it works, pay attention to when the mind sabotages it (this happens A LOT), follow the GPS system anyway (if you dare and are brave). All this is an experiment, and if it works and you are in a life of success, satisfaction, awe, peace, it will all be worth it.

So, even though I will say this is your decision-making process, if you follow it, it will lead you to a friggin fantastic life: you still might not be able to follow it.

This brings me to, why? How insane is that? Why would we sabotage a life we love? Well, the reason why is because the mind has cast a spell on society, and we have given it extreme power. So, when I tell you, it is not your mind you are listening to, relying on, and not giving it the power to control your life, but it is super limited, the mind will throw a complete tizzy-fit. So, let's chat about the MIND for one second before we go any deeper into this conversation about your unique decision-making strategy.

The mind has played its role in our human evolution and has uplifted humanity. We learned how to use tools, make fire, conquer nature, and then create money, democracies, cities, banking, food systems, homes. The mind has done amazing things for the growth of humanity. And yet, its time has come to an end, and it has reached its peak capacity. It is terrific for thinking, sharing, writing, learning, and communicating, but according to this system, it is outdated in making a decision.

According to this system, we are transcending the mind. We are awakening to a more advanced heightened decision-making process, a vehicle intelligence that is profoundly more advanced than the mind. Four hundred liters of blood per hour one hundred thousand times in one day is being pumped through your body, and no one is acknowledging this extraordinary life force intelligence running through our bodies.

This vehicle intelligence is leading us to a more evolved life, a visionary expression, a transcendent experience, if you are willing to let it. However, we all know how nuts the mind can be and how convincing. I will also recommend specific tools to help conquer the craziness of the mind as we continue. The mind talks inside the head; repeats backstories, runs through old memories, tells us how stupid we sound or ugly we look, tries to get us to act out emotionally, or ruminates on a recent drama. Basically, the mind uses our voice and makes us believe we should listen to all this madness. Not just listen but act on it. Some people are so wrapped up in this mind chatter, they don't even realize it is there. When they try and listen to the mind talking, they think there is no mind chatter; that it is just me. But, I am here to tell you that MIND CHATTER INSANITY is not the truth of who you are.

Now to transcend this power the mind has on us, this must

be ringing true for you deep down, and you must be willing to take this wild ride. You may have already noticed how your mind keeps you up at night, chases down the next shiny object, or forces you to do things it thinks you should do. You know you have, deep down, been longing to find a new way. Once you feel the truth in this, you will have a more profound inner conviction not to let the mind take over. It does take time; this is indeed the path of the mystic. Yes, it sounds familiar because many ancient mystery school teachings imbue techniques on transcending the mind. So we have known for a long time the limitations of the mind, and that it is not easy to conquer the mind chatter. These new tools will give you the direct support you need for this journey and your unique power source for decisions that you can rely on. So, Ra Uru Hu often stated that he believed this information was more for the parents who embodied this knowledge to pass on to their children. This way, we could unburden the new generations with the deep conditioning we all experienced. He often discussed most people are so inundated in their minds that very few would have the courage to dismantle the conditioning of the planet they were born with. So he encouraged more than anything to assist the children, so they don't suffer in the same way we did. I don't know about you, but I would like to prove him wrong on one of these points. I believe we all have within us, regardless of age, access to the profound courage it takes to dislodge the habitual thinking and patterns most of us have come to believe as truth.

There is something else besides the mind that will lose its power grip on you and might not like it. This is any teacher, guru, coach, or tribe that is controlling the way you think and the decisions you make. The minute you pull your power back from any authority you have given that power to, they are going to be super annoyed. Be it the church, your family, your partner, the priest, the rabbi, the job, the boss, the university, the professor, the media, the government, the group you are in, if they are low vibe, they will be super angry and not too accepting of this new you. By surrounding yourself with people who are willing to let you BE YOURSELF, this will be no problem at all. That is when you know you are around extraordinary people. Unfortunately, most people in society don't want to give up their control over you – just FYI.

But for now – let's explore your unique Inner Authority and how you are designed to make a decision AS YOU. Then we can talk about the power, courage, and internal commitment it will take to follow it.

Now I would like to ask that before we begin, you make a commitment to experimenting with this for at least 30 days. If you want to jump into our Facebook Community for support with this, we will be there for you! Check out the PDF for the link.

Inner Authority: The Unique GPS Systems

Your Inner Authority is like having personalized navigation. You don't have to think, and it guides you to the perfect locations, people, business moves, jobs, houses, partners, relationships, and even the right foods to eat. The crazy thing here is that once we GET IT, that we were all designed to make decisions differently, the world just gets a whole friggin lot simpler. Think about the choices we face every day, from the biggies to simple questions like where to go for dinner. To the annoying ones, like, what brand to buy at the supermarket. We face so many questions each day, some with great and grave circumstances.

There are so many options on making these decisions that it is nuts! So throw away any list-making, tarot cards, psychics that you go to, or anyone else that used to make your decisions, and pull up your sleeves and make a commitment to follow your OWN AUTHORITY, and let's see what happens. Perhaps you are on the precipice of a new magical land.

Probably the most critical piece of information that NO OTHER system gets right. I know this is a bold claim. There are many excellent systems out there, and many offer extremely useful tools; however, yes, I believe nothing helps differentiate each unique way of decision-making like this system. It is quite literally a complete game-changer in the self-help world.

This Inner Authority alone could change your life if you try it! If you have clients, it could change their lives as well.

There are a couple of different Types of Inner Authorities, and I will list them below.

Remember, these are far more detailed and nuanced than the description below. Also, it is different for each person. It usually takes a lot of time to really understand this in practice. I teach days on each one of these, and every person integrates it and experiences it differently. I will give you some suggestions on how to begin your experiment with your unique Authority here. Then, I suggest again turning to our PDF for more in-depth assistance on each of these and how to put it into practice.

All Authorities come into play after the Strategy. So, after you RESPOND, after you are INVITED, after you have waited for an entire moon cycle – then you listen to the Inner Authority to see if that is the right Invitation or the right thing to respond to. For a Manifestor, it is a little different because you don't really have to wait, so the Strategy and Authority will go hand and hand with informing. Like I said, it takes a little practice, a lot of Deconditioning, and some experience. Then one day, you are living in joy, satisfaction, ease, grace, success, and wonder you never thought possible. It sounds delish and too good to be true, but it is!

Inner Authorities

Emotional: As an Emotional Being, the most important thing to know is you need to feel your emotions entirely before making a rash decision (or any decision). When you are feeling the depth of your feelings, your life experience turns multidimensional and deep.

Most people are trained to stuff these puppies down. So, the first step for the Emotional Being is to learn to feel everything and feel it fully. Then make sure you don't assign a meaning or story to your emotions. Oh, I am down because Jerry just spoke to the kids in a nasty tone, or Susie just said I was a horrible monster for being late to her party. Of course, these things affect the emotions, but the idea here is just to feel emotions without the narrative chronicling of events. So, the next most important part of this is not to make any quick decisions. Go deep, process fully, let the emotions ride up and ride down, go through the entire wave. You will never get 100% yes or no, but after you go through the highs and lows, you will get pretty close. You will know what is a yes and what is a no through feeling and experimenting. Things to know, there is no truth in the now for you; if you wait at least 24 hours, your decision may go through a variety of yeses and no's. Usually first thing in the morning in the stillness, you will get about a 77% clarity on the right choice. Do not let anyone put pressure on you to be spontaneous or make quick decisions. If you feel like you are more of a Spock type with no emotions, this is very common and quite normal at first until this IA (Inner Authority) Type gives itself the freedom to FEEL. These beings have been taught to repress their emotions, so it may have shocked you to learn you are "Emotional." SIDE NOTE: while most people are in their Not-Self, the Emotional beings will feel more calm and subdued maybe a little sad, and the Undefined Emotional, more on this soon, will be bouncing off the walls in hysterical anxiety or depression. This is because of the amplification process the Undefined Centers experience. If this is the case for you, that your IA is Emotional, but no one would ever guess you shed a tear in your life, then you are in for a wild ride; it's time to unleash the floodgates! If you dare!

If you decide not to, pay attention and notice if people around you are out of control emotionally. If you witness a lot of drama and think it has nothing to do with you because you are so calm, think again.

Some of you feel your feelings; you have very high highs and low lows; if you are Emotional, this is actually healthy! The trick is not making a story about it and not making a decision from a high point in your wave. *WOO HOO, I feel so good; that house looks terrific. I am buying it now!* Or your low point in the wave, i.e., *I am so low, life sucks, I am going to sell all my belongings and live on an Ashram.* My advice to you is, don't do it! Ride out the highs and lows before acting on anything!

Also, please note that you are automatically Emotional Inner Authority if you have the Solar Plexus Defined. The Emotional wave is so powerful it trumps everything else in the chart.

Sacral: Very different from the Emotional Being. If the world just understood this one little tip, we could solve all of the world's problems, OK *many* of them. So Sacral is in the moment and is based on what we call Sacral Sounds. This is not something that is intuitive; you must retrain yourself to hear your own sounds. Highly recommend you turn to our PDF on this one to learn more deeply how to listen to the Sacral, then rely on it to guide your actions after RESPONDING. The Sacral makes these sort of grunt sounds. So, if someone asks you a yes/no question, don't use your mind, drop it down deep in the cavern of the gut and let a primordial sound happen that will be kind of like uh-hugh (yes) or un/nu (no). But these sounds are super personal, and they have to come out of you spontaneously. For many people, it feels like an expansion (for yes) or a closed feeling (for no). Experimenting is the best way to find out how these sounds will operate for you. Just a couple of notes. This is not what many people would refer to as: "listening to your intuition." This is much different. Maybe more like listening to your gut, but what happens for most people is the mind gets involved in answering the question. The minute you start to think, the Sacral response has left the building. Also, it is super hard for the Sacral to respond when people ask you open-ended questions. So, if you are trying to decide whether to go back to school or not, people should ask if it feels good for you to go back to school. So you can answer with a yes or a no sound. You don't want questions like, how do you feel about all the options for your next choice in life? Do you think you would prefer an internship, going to school, or getting a job? These are too many choices to ask a Sacral Being at once. You want to have someone ask pointed single-concept at a time, yes or no questions. Ideally, you want to have someone else ask you questions. If you are trying to write it out alone, the mind will take hold of that pen and have a field day. So, you want to avoid that and try to get direct, no/ yes through grunts. Don't let anyone ever tell you, "No, honey, use your words." You are designed to grunt.

Now, please notice how different the Sacral Being and the Emotional Being are. Yes, they indeed might both be powered by the Sacral in the case of any Emotional Generator or Manifesting Generator. Yet, one is fast in the moment, knowing and can make quick decisions. The other is glacial in its response and should be slow and deep and respected as such. We are different, and noticing these differences can help heal the world, the children, and at the very least, your next life choice!!

Splenic: The Splenic Inner Authority is what I have. It took me a super long time to understand how this one operates. The Spleen does not correspond to the Chakra system, and no, it is not felt in the actual Spleen. So, yes, at first, when someone tells you that the magical GPS system that will solve all your problems is in the Spleen, it's like WTF, how am I ever going to understand that? Trust me; I get it. And, unfortunately, this one does take a little bit longer to sense. This is an energy throughout the whole body in the lymphatic system. It is like having miniature sensors in each of the areas where the lymphatic system operates. It is an all-over body sensation. It is quick like a hummingbird; it is so fast that if you have thought about an answer, you missed the whole enchilada. You have to be in the silence and let this Spleen guide. It takes practice and faith that a lot of people before you have successfully discovered this. But, you can't just listen to their story and expect it will be the same for you. It is about slowing down, really listening, and letting *your* inner Spleen direct you. They say it is very subtle and a little harder to hear at first. However, many people who have mastered this say they almost feel a GONG going off in the right direction. Others have expressed that their Spleen lights up for them or just clicks into place for a yes, and gives a complete body shutdown for a no. For me, it just moves me in a direction without any thought. For example, if I lose my keys, I just follow where my body is driving me, and bingo, keys are found, without the mind telling me where to look.

When I work, I just let my Spleen direct what I do and when without my mind dictating its direction. So, as you can see, it is very different for different people. Again, check our PDF to go a little deeper. The Spleen does eventually become loud and clear as a GPS, so don't stress if this sounds outrageous at this point. Believe me, I was with you on this one. I could not for the life of me understand what they meant by listening to the Spleen. I studied and learned everything about Human Design before the Spleen made itself known to me. It took me so long because of my spiritual background; I was indoctrinated to listen to my heart, intuition, or channel my guides for direction. I trained myself to hear these things and follow them, but I honestly had no idea precisely what these things were. They were super inconsistent for me, and practically they always guided me into the wrong places. So, although the Spleen took a while to perk up in my inner guidance system, when it did, I could surrender into its wisdom because it worked like a trusted friend directing me so wisely. It always shocked me with its accuracy, with the beautiful success it was unfolding in my life, and the perfection of timing and direction it began to offer.

Ego Authority: Now for the Ego IA, this one really could follow the motto, follow your heart. Mind you, this is the ONLY IA that should follow that advice. And with how ubiquitous that saying is, this is a super rare Inner Authority with only around 4% of the population. (These numbers vary based on the number of charts that have been run.)

But, think about it, there is a tiny percentage of the population where this particular guidance would work. You have Ego Projectors and Ego Manifestors, and they both operate very differently. My point, following your heart just isn't the best advice out there AT ALL.

So, the Ego Center is also called the Will Power or Heart Center, so you can go after what it is that you want; let your heart guide you but be sure and learn your particular Strategy first, this makes a big difference. With the Ego Inner Authority, you want to have a healthy aligned EGO and focus on what is good for you, what feels like it lights up your heart. Do not push your will onto others. A healthy Will empowered, aligning to proper Strategy, will lead you to a life you love. Those with this Center that use it to push their agenda onto others are actively misusing this sacred energy. We see this a lot out there with the *come on you can do it* mottos of the world. For parents pushing their agenda onto children, this will cause a substantial cataclysmic backlash by any child. This Will Power is ONLY to be used to support your own heart. To move in the direction of the things YOU love. Not to push what you want onto anyone else.

As I mentioned, you might have an Ego Manifestor or an Ego Projector with this GPS System. These two beings are very different creatures and will have to operate uniquely with this same Inner Authority. So, the basic rule of thumb is to remember your Strategy first. Projectors, you will have to wait for an invitation and then feel into this invite. If it feels like something you would love to do, then it might be perfect for you! You have energy, you are recognized, you love it, a clear sign the Heart/Ego/Will is singing. For my Ego Manifestors, you have to feel into what you love first, then you INFORM (your Strategy), and then you can take peaceful, calm action. If you are frantic or out of alignment, this might not be a peaceful choice. Check in if you are in love. It all feels like a soothing peace-fest, and then after you inform there are loads of people who want to help you, and watch everything unfold perfectly. You might begin action and there are many obstacles in your path. You won't know if it is the right action until after you move forward so, if it isn't working out, check-in again with the heart and wait for the right inspiration. This Ego Center is notoriously known for being very trapped by the lure of the Ego, in the most unflattering terms. Meaning if you are focusing on getting ahead and revealing in the haves vs. the have nots, then your direction of Will might still be leading you astray. Healthy aligned Ego drive comes with time and Deconditioning.

Self-Directed: You will only see Projectors with this Authority. This IA is a Projector with a Defined G-Center (and Undefined Spleen, Sacral, Emotional, Ego), which is the Center for self, for direction, and for identity. Those with this GPS might need a little practice in understanding how this operates for them. One of the most important things for a Projector to be in touch with the SELF is to Decondition. This is a process I will be talking about in more depth, but basically, it is the journey of dismantling the Not-Self. Again this is huge for this GPS System because Projectors are run by the Generator world and think they are Generators for most of their lives. So, in order to have a healthy sense of self, you must shed everything you thought you were. After this shedding takes place, your Inner Authority has to do with knowing who you are and making sure that everything you do perfectly reflects the truth of YOUR UNIQUENESS. It has to do with making sure your decisions reflect things that reflect your values, what you believe in, what has authenticity for you.

You might need a sounding board to hear your voice process the thoughts while trying to make a decision. A sounding board is a nonjudgmental person willing to listen with no advice when you BLAH. You know what BLAH means, right? Just let it all come out, speak about what you might gain or lose from the choice you are pondering. Explore the possibilities, the good, the bad, the ugly of all directions. Feel the frequency of the BLAH. When you speak, you will feel a resonance to your sound that feels correct for you. So some questions to ask are, is this me, does this decision represent me? Will this job reflect my truth, my values, or how I understand myself? The Self-Directed will begin to get clear on this as they have a trusted, non-biased person to listen to them talk it out, then bingo, the right decision will pop out for you and reflect who you are perfectly. No, this isn't easy; this is a more complicated and rare Inner Authority. But, as you practice and get comfortable in who you are, what makes you unique, and learn to honor and respect this, the beauty of you will unfold.

Environmental Authorities:
Often These Two Are Referred to as NONE

These two have a little different essence to them. They can still be used to make decisions, but they take a little more time to master and experiment with. They are called None because primarily, these people are here for other people, to provide them with wisdom and awareness. Often I have also seen these called Outer Authorities; the distinction is everyone has an

Outer Authority, which I will explain in greater detail below.

Mental/None: The only people with this Authority will be Projectors. The Projector with Mental Authority will have outstanding knowledge for those people around them once they master their systems and learn how to live as a Projector. When making a decision, it will help them to have an outside sounding board, similar to the Self-Projected IA, someone who can just listen until the frequency becomes very clear for them about the right decision. So, it will just sound *off frequency* until you hit on the right choice for you as you speak. BINGO, your frequency, the tone will reflect the right choice. I know this sounds cryptic, almost impossible to understand at first. I have worked with several Projectors who have mastered this. After a lifetime of torture, this little bit of knowledge assisted in their ability to make correct decisions for their life. The environment is essential because there is so much openness in these charts. In a way, if you aren't in the right place, if it feels off to you for any reason, then it might be harder to make decisions. So, your environment is a vital piece for you. So be sure and feel good where you are living.

There are many aspects to this Mental IA. You are very open. Usually, you will have the Head, Ajna, and maybe the Throat Center defined. This means you are absorbing and amplifying the outside world in most of your Centers, and it can be very confusing and overwhelming for this Type. Deconditioning is a massive part of the journey for the Mental Projector; they are here to lead, guide, and direct with their wisdom and fantastic advice for other people. However, to uncover their genius, it's a process of unraveling all the conditioning, learning to find the right frequency as they speak so they can sort through the correct invitations. Once this is mastered, they have super vital work to do in the world! The weather or transits (meaning how the neutrino stream is moving through with the placement of the planets) might significantly affect your decision-making. Davidian has some great intel on this, and we will have this available for you on our PDF if you are a Mental Projector and need more support.

Lunar Authority: This is just for those who are Reflectors, and Reflectors need a particular way of dealing with their uniqueness.

They are the Unicorns of the Human Design world. They reflect the world around them, and if they are healthy and vibrant often, they are reflecting two things: that they are in the right place, and if the business/home/relationship they are in is thriving and healthy. If you are in a working environment, for example, that is toxic for you, it is time to exit.

It takes time to make decisions, a full lunar cycle. Hence the name – you are very connected to the moon. Don't let the world rush you. The Lunar Authority will witness the entire 28-day lunar cycle and let the decision percolate the entire month. It helps to have a journal and keep track of how you are sensing about the decision each day. You can also notice the transits moving through your chart; it will light up certain hanging Gates and create a Channel for you. This Channel may help you receive a little more understanding of the energy passing through your system throughout your cycle. Learning this cycle for you, what Gates are lit up and when can support you in making choices. The environment is essential for you as well, as we have mentioned before. If you are in the right place, decisions just get more precise and more accessible. If you are in the wrong or a toxic environment, even if you wait a full month, you might have difficulty making the right choice. So, again, being in the right place that feels good to you is a BIG KEY!

In conclusion, this personalized GPS System is an incredible tool! **Now** you will always be with the right people, towards the right career, in the right place! That is a little overly simplistic.

However, this is the idea. We all have a majestic divine role to play, and our vehicle intelligence has far more brilliance to guide us than the mind's limited ability. Now, do you have the courage to listen to your Authority and not let your mind, your social conditioning, or your fears tell you what to do? Notice how you take on the experiment and decide to listen to your unique GPS and how the mind will resist. Notice also how much power our society has placed on the mind as the king of all intelligence. The intellect is revered in our culture. Yet social intelligence, emotional intelligence, divine intelligence, connection to spirit, the kindness of people's hearts, which are all far more potent intelligence, are actually looked down upon in our society. Connection to the vehicle intelligence and releasing the grip of the intellect will assist you in transcending the mind.

Let's explore how you will notice the mind play out in your own life, for example. Your Inner Authority will say yes to a brand new career opportunity or job that is correct for now but different from what you have, but the mind will say something like... *"Are you nuts? We have been in this career for years, we are good at it, it is stable, we get the 401k, no companies are this great... nice try... but no."*

Or you might hear something like, "This friendship/family member/relationship is draining you," and you get a YES – to move on. Your mind will say something like, *"Well, this person has been in my life for 20 years, I can't say no to a lunch date, or not return their calls."* Your Inner Authority is getting the YES TO MOVE ON, yet the mind will resist it for a myriad of reasons. This battle is basically the inner struggle that you will probably experience for a while until the Inner Authority time and time again proves its validity.

You don't have to leave anything dramatically without kindness, but sometimes, if your Inner Authority is guiding you in new directions, it is super imperative to act per that guidance.

So, it all sounds simple enough; however, my beautiful friend, whom I honor so much as if you are here, listening, and willing, it is not easy. Honor the path and the warrior spirit to just say YES to the journey.

Outer Authority

Just a little clarification on the Outer Authority. It is often said the Mental and Lunar Authority are more of an Outer Authority. This means that most of their process, once they have De-conditioned, is for other people. Their insights, their reflections will serve the other. However, they do often struggle with finding out how to make decisions for themselves, so I like to assist in this clarification.

Another point is that we all have Outer Authority. This is when the mind has become free from the conditioning of making decisions for "the life." The mind then becomes an agent of wisdom, based on one's particular Design, for other people. This is a liberation process, a transcendence of the mind's current state. When the Inner and Outer Authority are working in true harmony and alignment, we see a person genuinely living as their unique self.

Chapter 9

Biz by Design

Without work, all life goes rotten. But when work goes soulless, life stifles and dies.
Albert Camus

Over the years of helping thousands of people learn about their unique Design and businesses, these are the questions I get asked the most:

- How do I live my Design and support myself financially?
- If I am just waiting for the invitation or responding, how do I start a business or change careers?
- How do I market or advertise if I am not here to initiate?
- If I am a Projector, what careers should I choose?
- What is the best job for my Type?

All of these questions fall into the category of Human Design Business. Meaning, how do you make money and talk about the actual bottom line while still being true to yourself?

Let's just say, when you realize you have been living as your Not-Self theme, this usually means you have been stuck in a career, job, or business that you don't love. Perhaps you were working somewhere because you felt you should, your parents thought it was a good idea, maybe it was a good living, or perhaps you are still in a career that suited an old version of you, but you are now burned out and ready for something more fulfilling.

If you are doing something that you hate, are frustrated, or feel like you are living on borrowed time, you feel fried to the bone: you may be living as your Not-Self. Just following your

Strategy and Inner Authority will help. However, there is more to your chart that can also help with business choices.

So, now that we have established this – NOW WHAT? Great question. So, let's chat about business.

I am a serial entrepreneur; I ran my first business right from my dorm room in college. It failed miserably, but hey, I was a youthful enterprising young girl, and that is all part of the territory.

My nature has always been to start businesses on my own. I pushed and shoved and followed several self-help Law of Attraction books, yet I still struggled to get them off the ground. Of course, there were plenty of wins: my first brick-and-mortar franchise was one of the top-grossing franchises in CA. We made over multiple 6-figures in the first year and sold the business for a quarter of million dollars after only two years. But again, aspects of myself in this business were not recognized, and snuffing them out to run the day-to-day stifled my truth and my true genius. Also, when I did have business wins, they were wrought with burnout and exhaustion. Although I sought out many tools to help me with business, I could never genuinely be myself and earn money. Many of my clients have felt this way too. This statement is just an FYI; this is by no means to discredit the inner work done with my Master's Degree work. I think that healing inner trauma and pain has to be done before anyone can truly live a successful and balanced life in business or any goal. Human Design really helps to understand where the trauma may be coming through Aura mechanically and how you react to it. It also provides you with perspectives unseen in therapy – the two work hand and hand, in my opinion. Sometimes, doing something like therapy or spiritual psychology like I did will be an additional tool to support the healing of any past traumas. If you do one without the other, there are serious issues that are missed. Humans are complex creatures. If you crave self-growth, self-actualizing, and living a life of great success and deep inner healing, release, forgiveness, and awakening, sometimes it does take some doing.

So, if you feel like you are capable of so much more than your current career, this section is for you. You know you are designed for greatness but have no idea how to get from an idea to manifest the career you were born for. This brings us to the focus of the Human Design business; part of my life mission is to serve others in this area because of the years of turmoil and torture I went through to figure this out for myself.

As I studied Human Design, I realized there was no more excellent map to guide people to businesses, careers, and jobs aligned to bring their soul joy because it assisted them in their PURPOSE. It was never exactly in the way people THOUGHT it would be. Unfortunately, you can't just give someone an A-to-Z plan to the soul's purpose. Instead, you must evolve into the person you know you were born to be through trials, through courageous action, through LIVING YOUR DESIGN, and then one day, BOOM, you are aligning in a career you love. Human Design will share with you how to do this in the world of business. As you have learned, Projectors are not here to initiate action with their goals, ideas, or even thoughts. When they do, there are extreme and dire consequences of the most uncomfortable kind. Yes, I am also an Undefined Emotional Being, so I tend to be a wee bit dramatic at times. But, it is true for many Projectors; they feel stymied about the business piece while learning to live their Design. I am here to tell you that everyone is here to "manifest" a life they love, the opus they were born to play out, even if they are not Manifestor Types in Human Design.

However, we all need to go about this actualization of our life in different ways. Thank goodness we now know this! You're Welcome!

In all seriousness, let me share a little about Human Design and Business with you, so you don't have to suffer as I did.

This is a super necessary conversation. I will give you the most important practical tools you can take with you right now and begin implementing in your life pronto.

This information is from the wisdom of the I Ching, one of the critical places Human Design was derived from, my years in Corporate America, my experience with my clients, my Human Design studies. I have experimented with all this intel in real live businesses, and put together a snapshot of how this might work best for you.

I just wish someone could have broken this down for me in a super simple, bite-sized way to understand how to implement this for success. I found the materials were super complicated to learn, not very practical, overly intellectualized, and not the same in theory as in practice. Hence, I have been called for the greater good of humanity to break this system down for you in a way more people will be able to utilize for their personal freedom in the arena of finances. Because haven't we all suffered long enough? No, you don't have to change the world or go out there and fight the government for any changes. What I am here to tell you is don't LOOK OUT THERE anymore. I am pointing to you and your INNER WIRING. I am saying look inside yourself for all the details. I will direct you, and once I do, don't ever look out into the world and think they have power over you or your life or direction again because they do not. This level of empowerment is so HUGE it is essential for my life purpose that I share it with as many people as possible. If anyone is trying to take away your power to make your own decisions in any way, shape, or form, they DO NOT have your best interests at heart.

My intention for this chapter is to give you super practical tools you can absorb right now so you can free yourself from a life of pain and suffering in jobs and careers that suck your blood.

Your life force is valuable; you don't have to give it over to

ANYTHING ANYMORE that is not correct for you. But how do we do this and learn to trust the Universe enough so we don't end up penniless or on the street? Another great question.

So, let's dive into it!

The most important thing to understand about this topic is that you are different when you are in business than when you are NOT. Yes, new skills, developments, and insights begin to flower in the business, job, or group dynamic that don't happen alone. This is such a critical point, so if you were zoning out or just did an Instagram post while reading this, go back and read that last sentence again. Or let me say it another way. When you are alone, you are one way; you become an entirely new 2.0 version of yourself in a business setting. Actually, this is true not only in a business setting but when you are with any other people. With one other person, you form a partnership dynamic; two charts come together and make a unique configuration; however, when you have three people who come together, you form a Penta. This Penta, is a very interesting beast that deserves much attention. It might just change how you view every get-together, family function, business meeting, networking event, or any time you are not alone.

I will be going over some of the business Channels of the Penta and the WA very briefly. If you would like a list of the overall Gates and Channels and the meanings of each of these, check out the supporting materials for this book on our website for the PDF: https://foxy5d.com/pages/are-you-a-mutant.

As you are starting in business or if you want support in making money, you do have to look at your chart in a new way. So, before he transitioned, the founder of Human Design, Ra Uru Hu, brought forward a new arena of Human Design; people called it Base Group 5. Basically, it was the body of knowledge that brought Human Design to Business.

However, Ra never really fleshed it out completely,

never followed it through with real-life examples, so anyone purporting to be the ONLY expert on this... quite frankly, is not. We are all living, breathing examples of the experiment.

We all had to take on this unfinished intel, experiment with it in real-time business (not just theory), apply it, and see what worked in the actual world of business.

The most important thing I can share with you now is that the business aspect is not something you get just by studying Human Design because it is so very different.

In the Human Design business arena, we look at how you operate in a group if you are designed to create a solo-preneurship, if you are designed to lead large corporations or operate in a small group. You will also uncover the skills that awaken when you are in a group.

The group dynamic operates in a Penta when there are more than three people or a WA when there are three Pentas, 16 people.

The Penta creates a Trans-auric entity and what this means is that when three people come together, something bigger is created, a literal ONE THING. So, everyone in the group feeds into this Penta, whether you like it or not. You know what they say. Be careful whom you surround yourself with. This is SO TRUE.

The Penta is a force that homogenizes the group. It forces people to be the same. It will not recognize the Individual, and it doesn't have self-awareness. At least at the time of writing this book, there is no self-awareness within the Penta. An unconscious Penta means that when any group of three or more people comes together for a project, they are unaware of the group dynamic. They are moving forward, creating a tribe of hive-minded people for a specific goal, and each of the individuals is unaware of how it operates within the group context.

This unconscious Penta is something according to RA that

will change during the 2027 mutation. The Penta will become more conscious; no one understands what this means exactly or how it will operate; the idea is the Aura Mechanics of a group will become more self-aware of the group connection. Ra seems to purport that he knew what this would look like, but only time will tell. I'm afraid I personally have to disagree with a lot of the specific prophecy by Ra on what exactly society will look like come 2027. Hence, why I find it essential to share the actual Aura Mechanics, my interpretation of what that means, and let you, the beautiful experimenter, decide by your own Inner Authority and contemplate for yourself. I do have a sense that the wheel shift will be a fantastic experience that I am looking forward to witnessing! I would rather be optimistic and discover after the end of the world I was wrong, then prophesize and commit to the vision of the apocalypse and be RIGHT, just saying. But let's face it, not one end of the world prophesy has come true, and there has been no shortage of them over the last 411 years.

You can contemplate this Penta energy or group dynamic by noticing the synthesis created when people come together in a team, group, business, office, or any collaboration. Once we move into the Era of the Individual or the Cross of the Sleeping Phoenix 2027, the group dynamic will become conscious of the energies, the emotions, the possible thoughts of the people in the group. There will be a sort of evolution of group-think or collective consciousness. Some people imagine this being like the series called *Sense8* on Netflix. This show was about a group of eight people in a pod who communicated telepathically; they could call on each other and use the superpower strengths of the other people in their pod if they needed them. I am not giving this show a rave review or telling you to go watch it. Nor am I claiming to know exactly what will happen as the Penta becomes more conscious. There have been many other ideas of what this might look like, but here is the truth. Does anyone ever really know the future? I have read through many of

Nostradamus' predictions, and a lot of things were based on the "if we do not evolve, we might go down this road." Still, no one has ever adequately predicted precisely what the future will look like unless I am grossly misevaluating all of our history's most excellent psychics due to knowledge I was not exposed to. From everything I have EVER read, all the 2012 prophecies or Y2K predictions, none of them came true, so I like to keep all possibilities open.

So, no, I do not adhere to anyone's prediction or prophecy on this. However, I do notice that when you study Aura Mechanics and see how the wheel is going to shift, there are insights to be gained. You can see the energies moving and contemplate how you will need to pivot and stay in the present moment, witnessing the shift and watching the movie unfold. The 2027 information is so accurate, and I will get more into this later.

So, with all of that said, we are moving toward a more conscious group dynamic, including organizations put together to make money. If you ponder a conscious group, it does sound a lot like what the mystics have been claiming for centuries about the evolved human capable of feeling oneness rather than separation.

In business, traditionally in our capitalistic culture, industries, and business organizations are the most unconscious establishments on a mission of self-service above all others. Watching them become more conscious could be very interesting; consciousness means awareness of how the means affect the ends. Conscious group dynamics might also mean the group becomes aware of how the top is fairly or unfairly treating the individual. Or how anyone in a group is bullying, unfairly treating, berating, victimizing anyone else in the group.

As of today, the unconscious group, the Trans-auric entity called the Penta, will move the group forward and treat everyone like a Generator, whether you are one or not. Every time you are with three people, you create a Penta. The perfect Penta is five people, four Generators, and one Projector acting as the Alpha or the group leader. The leader is supposed to be outside the Penta to lead, guide, and direct the group's energy. It makes sense. Projectors have a remarkable ability to see where the power or energy is being misused or might be too busy for substantial results. In a perfect Penta, the group recognizes this leading force as a beautiful light to direct them. However, this means that the leader should work fewer hours and not be made to feel like a lazy good for nothing for leaving the office at 1:00pm and sleeping in a little longer than the rest. We might see this with some leadership, but in most cases, if you are a CEO or running a company, you are expected to work long hours, work harder, hustle, and not sleep. So as a collective, we have some evolution to do to form a perfect Penta in action.

Of course, if you are an entrepreneur, you are the boss or the CEO of a company. This is your opportunity to be on the leading edge with this intel. This means if you have a Projector in your company, they can still be a leader even if they work less and sleep more. No, they are not lazy or less than. OK, now that we have that mapped out, we can evolve as a species.

Once we have a small business that grows into a company that includes more than six people, you then need to have two separate Pentas. If you are developing as a small business and moving into a larger company making sure you have Pentas with 12 skills is very important. So, sometimes it is better to keep the Penta as it is until you have a great group to form a second Penta before you hire on one or two people.

Have you ever noticed how just one more person throws off the energy of the group? It changes things. It is not just that person. It is the entire Aura Mechanics of the group!

Crazy right? We have all experienced this in the past. So, ideally, you have three perfect Pentas before you pop into a WA, which is 16 people; once you move into the WA, three Pentas plus one leader, the dynamic shifts AGAIN! Entirely new aspects of the chart begin to TURN ON! This means depending on your chart: you might thrive in larger or smaller businesses. If you have one of the six WA channels, you might thrive in a big company.

As we are already noticing the breakdown of many industries, people will be looking for new directions, new ways of working together, new ideas to be efficient. Adding Human Design as the personal assessment tool on high-vibe steroids helps you understand each person's unique ability to drive the business forward if they are given the freedom to operate as themselves within the context of the group, business, or company.

The industries, corporations, and how we have made money are not as stable as they once were, and truth be told, it isn't sound at all. Many small businesses have closed their doors due to the Pandemic; many people are struggling and ready to create a new way to bring in money.

When things fall apart, new systems can be built. You can see these times as a sort of revolution – an entirely new way to see money-making, business building, and teamwork development. These Human Design tools, in my opinion, will revolutionize the world of business.

Imagine a time where the keys to ALL shackles are given to all the people. No one needs to work in a job or career they don't enjoy. Imagine a time when no one HAS TO/SHOULD DO/OR DOES anything ever again that is not right for them, and everyone around agrees. WOWZA, right? No one pressures you to do what they think/know/or demand that you should do. Because everyone knows that when each person follows what is right for them as the magic of a beehive, we are all driven to the excellent work we are designed for, and that magically plays the perfect part in the Universal Puzzle. We all acknowledge and allow each other to work and live based on this principle. Imagine if everyone lived according to their own genius, how they were designed to work in the business. What if everyone knew they had innate skills, and they performed them with JOY! The big and small enterprises agreed when they worked this way, employees were happy, healthy, more productive, and the BEST part, you can rest assured your company, big or small, will be more profitable. Imagine if these were the truths we lived by. You think the world might feel a little nicer? I do. As we speak, or as I am writing this, we are experiencing the great walkout; employees are quitting in droves. I see this as absolutely part of this shift in Aura Mechanics. Once we get closer and closer to the wheel turning, it will make it almost impossible for people of power to make individuals do things against their own personal well-being anymore. This shift in dynamics just might be a big problem for large industries if they do not change their ways. You can see why learning and implementing the basics of these tools is important, regardless of whether you are running a one-person operation or a sizeable multifaceted industry.

Imagine we saw the potential in each other, empowered this potential so each person could thrive as themselves regardless of race, sex, color, creed, or body type. Anything short of this is still in the archaic dark ages.

Feel it; this has power!

No one needs to work in a job or career they hate, no one needs to do what they are not designed to do, and no one person is meant to be in servitude to another for money against their will. Or, for that matter, no one should put their will onto the sovereign Inner decision-making Authority of another person, PERIOD. Let that sink in. Not for the greater good of the whole, not for the sake of any ends; this intel gives no one the power to infringe their will onto another person.

If we are set free, would we work at all? Would everyone just have a free for all and play video games all day?

Great questions! According to our Design, the answer is YES, people would work and thrive in their passion, doing skills they were born for, and would ALL (yes all of you) THRIVE in their work! This could be anything from housework, teaching, running a tech company, singing in a band, being an online entrepreneur, a writer, whatever you feel called to do. It might change over time as well; those days of sticking to one career for a lifetime are archaic. We are designed to do effervescent living work (constantly changing and never static) globally, doing what we love to do, which feels satisfying and enjoyable. We are all capable and designed to work in a career, job, or business that empowers us naturally to thrive. We are also abundant in nature when we remove constraints, control, power, wounding, self-doubt, we are all equally valuable creatures, and our true source is infinite. So, yes, a world where everyone is thriving in their unique expression, doing work they love, and making substantial money for all opens the door to a visionary world. It really isn't visionary according to Human Design; it is our true divine-human nature. Such a simple concept. So how did this get this so friggin screwed up in our culture?

This section will go over some business mechanics based on Human Design and some pure inspiration that I hope to instill in you. If you don't like what you do, there is always time to live out your true-life purpose. Or if life-purpose feels like an ambitious undertaking, let's just say that you might just walk away feeling you do not need to settle for a job, career, lifestyle, business that burns you out or doesn't indeed provide satisfaction. But, remember your first step is always to WAIT. If you learn one thing from this system, patience, regardless of the #hustle Starbucks-infused culture we are in, is a virtue – one to be honed and mastered.

Because most of the population are still somewhat slaves to paying the bills, what this generally means is that we are also slaves to our fears. Believe me, I know this all too well. As I was contemplating leaving Corporate America, I would have panic attacks about making enough money. I was terrified I would not be able to support myself, then become unemployable, and I would lose my house. The fear was so tangible in my body it rippled like a roaring fire in my belly, demanding I stay stuck.

Why are we so afraid and so controlled by the mortgage, paying our bills, and having a good life, that we sacrifice our well-being, our joy, our time, often our health to get to work?

I was so curious about this. Primarily because I did it too, for an entire decade working for Corporate America. Well it was only the last three years I became dull, uninspired, and anxious. Still, I stayed for those three years and was tortured by it. I was in pain, unhappy, bored, and I would say things like, "I hate my life," when I would wake up in the morning... and yet... I was too afraid to leave, so I stayed.

I had so many excuses as to why I should stay. The myriad of excuses would be, I like it here, I know how to do it, I am good at it, people love me, I make great money, I am in a good situation, I work from home, I have it easy, not too many hours. It went on and on. I was terrified literally of not having a paycheck.

I knew I was meant for so much more! I knew I had creative fire and inspiration in me, but my blade was being dulled so that I could pay the mortgage. It seemed easier to take risks in your twenties or thirties because you have time. I had taken risks in the past, and they caused me so much pain.

In your forties, and for me, it was well into the 40s (no need to go into full details on this one). Let us just say it is more complex when your mind also thinks you should be rational, prepare for your retirement; you can't recreate your life at 40 etc., etc. But you can. You can begin at any age to live your dream one small step at a time.

So, these are some of the things that have brought me to where I am now... my story in my career. Do you have your story? Because I have now worked with hundreds of women entrepreneurs, and let me tell you, I have heard A LOT of stories.

I have heard a lot of women blaming others for their situation, being afraid to move forward, feeling entitled because they paid you $997.00 for a course that they should already have a booming business. I get it, I have felt that way too. With all the advertising and marketing, it is so darn confusing how to have a business and convert that business into serious high income rather than a hobby. It is no wonder we think if we take a course, get a certification, that then we should have a multi-six-figure business. But, often, in almost every case I have witnessed, it is just not that simple. Most entrepreneurs go through a journey of highs and lows, pitfalls and failures, deep perseverance before settling into success. Regardless of your Human Design Type! However, when you know your Design, you not only have a huge leg up in your own career, you have an advantage if you are any type of business, life, relationship coach. Or you serve clients on any level. Knowing this detail can divert much suffering.

So, now this brings me to another piece of the business puzzle.

I am going to introduce you to the most effective assessment tool on the planet. Combining ancient and modern-day sciences, we are using the power of Human Design to crack the business code. It may not bring that instantaneous success, but it just might make the road a little smoother and a heck of a lot more enjoyable.

So, let's get cracking the business code!

When you understand your inner Business by Design Success Code, here are a couple of things that start to become evident in business:

- What business skills do you innately have? (Hint, this might not be what you are trained in.)
- Who in your company is a good fit and why?

- Are you losing integrity in the marketplace? Learn the secret ingredient.
- Do you wonder why your clients might not feel like they trust your company?
- Do you always hire the same types of people?
- Do you have a high turnover?
- Are you having luck in getting your product or programs into the right hands?
- Do you need a boost in sales?
- Marketing techniques that won't bring crickets.
- How to keep ahead of trends.
- Why your accounting might always be off.
- How to hire the exact right team.
- Are you designed to be a solopreneur?
- Do you have what it takes to lead a large company or to run your own small business?

Quite literally, all of the above issues are read… wait for it… in your DNA coding – your Human Design chart.

So, like I said, imagine if we knew why some people could handle 12-hour days and others could not; imagine if we eliminated burnout? Imagine we put every person on your team (or in the world for that matter) in their zone of genius.

What if I said I was going to break this down for you in a few simple steps?

OK, this is a complex science, but I will break it down for you in the most straightforward direct path possible. Starting with the two most important steps to begin this process and, of course, give you the possibility of jumping down the rabbit hole if you want more ingenious intel on our website for the book's bonus materials.

The first two most critical simple steps are:

1. Cracking your Success Code. Your Type and Strategy for

you!
2. Learn how you were designed to make decisions. Your Inner GPS!
3. YUP, I already covered steps 1 and 2!
4. Next, it is about learning everything else about your chart. ☺Joking! I am just breaking down the essential tips. But knowing we have already covered the first two key factors means you already know more than most of the workforce!

Your Aura in business has a specific nonverbal communication always going on, yes, even over ZOOM. When you enter into a room, your Aura speaks; your Aura invites or pushes people away or invites people to ask you for information. Your Aura has a way of interacting with other people.

Your business has a Trans-auric field. Whenever there are more than two people who come together for any type of business, you create something more significant than the individual.

Each individual has a role to play in a group. Oh, but guessing what that role is, is so darn confusing because the mind is chaotic and quite frankly confused most of the time.

This drive to succeed in business is a significant desire many people want. Yet, so many companies never achieve this. They might have success for a while but not be able to compete or keep up. This is also very true for start-ups or people trying to launch a new business venture of their own. It can be far more complicated than any Facebook or YouTube ads will let on.

Business success is still pretty rare, especially with small business start-ups. There are ways to uncover critical business secrets, and the power to understand who you are in the realm of business is at your fingertips.

So, here are the first places to start with this. Each Aura Type has a different role in the Penta.

The Aura Types in Human Design Business

The Generators, including the Manifesting Generators – These Types are here to do work they love. You can call these Types Classic Creative Dynamos (Generators) and Speedy Creative Dynamos (Manifesting Generators), those who are here to be DOING WORK THEY LOVE! Their purpose is to work in satisfying careers. Simple insight, if you are a Generator or a Manifesting Generator and you are doing work you hate that drives you nuts, drains you, or burns you out, you are not aligning with your true-life purpose. And yes, you have a purpose, and yes, your work should reflect it. Even if you do housework, raise children, act in plays, whatever you are doing, you should feel satisfied. You are designed to operate within a Penta, and really you are the best Type to be in a Penta. Of course, there are more clarifying aspects to who will love small groups or smaller type companies.

However, the Generators and Manifesting Generator Dynamos are here to make up the bulk of the working and creative force of the Penta.

Projectors – These Types of Auras are the leaders of the pack. Or, what I like to call Expert Consultants who are here to lead, guide and direct the energy of the Penta. If you are working an incredibly draining job and are not allowed to delegate or direct others, you might not be in the work you were designed for. If you are feeling extremely burned out or overworked, if you initiated to get where you are, you might be bitter in your current position. If you think no one gets you or listens to you, you might not be in exemplary work. But, if you follow your Strategy and wait to be invited or recognized, you will be led to the proper position for you. It is a wonderful reminder you are designed to do something that inspires you and does not destroy you or burn you out. Even though not everyone recognizes you, here is a little critical and juicy fact about the Projector. You can do a nine-hour workday in two hours because you know every shortcut, and you get it done fast, as long as you are not drained, exhausted, or beaten down. You are here to master systems while you wait for recognition; you must get good at something, and you will get seen for it. As a Projector, you need to be a little better than most but have no fear, you will master something you love. Remember, regardless of what anyone says about the poor Projector, you are here to thrive in the workplace, to succeed in what you love, to be leaders, to run the joint in a loving but bossy pants way, asking all the right pointed questions to get the most out of the team.

You are here to guide and direct, to see what needs to be done and let people know.

Oversee, coach, teach, lead; you are here to ask the right questions and point people in the right direction.

Technically, Projectors, you are the Alphas, and you are supposed to be in charge and do so only working a couple of hours a day. Hallelujah!

But how? You ask! Well, this is something we genuinely haven't figured out yet as a culture. Projectors, it is up to you to be progressive, make change, and lead the revolution towards new ways to act and be in your careers. You are here to see higher methods with differing perspectives. You have striking insights if adequately recognized and invited for your genius. You can make Revolutionary changes in forward-thinking companies and businesses. Think of the very first African American President of Hope, Obama, a great example of a forward-thinking Projector. His presidency marked an entire shift in thinking in this country; it was revolutionary for his progressive leadership. Not getting political or looking at his failures or practices, just the archetypal figure as a leader, Projector. He knew how to revolutionize some serious outdated and backward thinking on who should be President.

Projectors/Advisors are here to be the Alpha of the Penta. They direct the energy and the direction of the Penta. Obama exemplified a new way to lead by pointing out and leaning on brilliant people to assist. He would recognize, call-out the genius in his team, then depend on them by delegating, and in return, they honored and recognized him as a revolutionary new type of leader. There are also tons of meme pictures of him sitting on the couch as he would give orders. Please let's not make this about political rightness/wrongness or red/blue. Just for the record, I am neither Republican nor Democrat and have chosen my entire adult life not to engage in politics at all by choice; my revolution is outside the system. So, don't get all bunched up in your political stuff.

Generators and Projectors have a magical agreement and are here to be in the Penta together. They make great business partners and are here to manifest magical businesses as teams.

There is a beautiful dynamic with these two Aura Types when everyone is operating correctly. They are technically the only Two Types that should be operating in a Penta. So this deserves a deep pause, Projectors and Generators have a mystical relationship and are here to do amazing things together.

Manifestors – I like to call this Type the Innovative Fire Starter. The rock gets thrown out by the Manifestor, creates ripples of creative source energy that we all get to ride on. The Manifestor has been in power here on the planet for a long time.

They have impact and force, and let's just say they performed a powerful job; well done. The Manifestor gets things started, the ball rolling, they know what needs to be activated. This fire-starter has a keen knowledge and skill. And they are almost ready to put their feet up and say, I am prepared for a peaceful retirement. However, of course, as a Manifestor, if you feel that you have been imploded not willing to initiate and awaken your Manifestor power, you will still need to do this first before you sit back and watch the wheel spin.

The JUST DO IT motto has worked for you for a long time but is finally coming into full recognition for the power it creates but only for a small portion of the population. We are moving into a world where the Projector, the wise one on the mountain, is here to provide insight, lead and direct the future mutation.

The Manifestor still has an influential role as the starter, and they can manifest their dreams. They feel, desire, speak it, then take action, and they start a wave of motion. They are to start companies, not here to run the company, so they need to rely on the Generators to do that and the Projectors to watch, view, direct, and guide the overall vision and process.

Now, remember, yes, I am a Projector, so although this is all true and I am not making this up, I am simply repeating back in my insightful fashion the words of Ra Uru Hu. So, it is he that has stated this transition is happening with the leadership passing of the torch for the 2027 mutation period. He himself was a Manifestor and was imagining a world of peaceful Manifestors beautifully watching the work they have done, leaning back lovingly watching the new leaders arise. If this makes you angry, I know it makes many Manifestors angry; remember, retirement only comes when you are ready after you have lived the many life manifestations you are here to awaken for your soul. Peace is the purest and high vibe frequency we all need on the planet right now, so know how vital and essential this incredible position is for the evolution of humanity.

The Manifestor is here to work outside the realm of the Penta by innovating new directions to get things started and designed as the Lone Wolf. Far too often, I see a Manifestor create something but get stuck in the daily grind. This routine of extended hours for the Manifestor spells massive burnout, so making sure you can delegate after you begin your new innovations is enormous for you to thrive! Far too often, I see Manifestors in business Pentas due to life and circumstances that might be super uncomfortable for them. So, check in how you feel when you are in a small business structure and are being conditioned to work as a Generator.

Reflector – I like to refer to them as the Biz Connoisseur in Human Design Business. The Reflectors are here to tell us where we are going awry and if the flavor of the project is off. The Reflector tells us how things in the company or business are running. Think canary in the coal mine.

A canary in a coal mine is an advanced warning of some danger. The metaphor originates from the times when miners used to carry caged canaries while at work; if there was any methane or carbon monoxide in the mine, the canary would die before the levels of the gas reached those hazardous to humans.
Wikipedia

So, think about this, the canary reflects the toxicity of the work environment to save the whole ship.

Super sensitive, the Reflector is here to reflect, taste, sample, and let us know what is happening in their environment. Finding a great career can be intense for this Type, but trust you are super important for the whole. You are so needed in business in the proper position. The perfect example of a famous Reflector is Michael Jackson, who reflected to us the health of the music industry. The superficial nature of this world he grew up in left him dying because he needed anesthesia to fall asleep, uppers to lift him up, and ultimately had so many plastic surgeries on his nose that when he was brought to the hospital, he had a hole where his nose was because the prosthetic fell off. He reflected the music industry was superficial, addicted, and pretty much a toxic world. Had he been in the right environment and done a little healing on himself, he would have represented the Unicorn of the Reflector. I know I will get a lot of hate for saying anything negative about the King himself (trust me I really held myself back), but you don't have to go far to research the greed, manipulation, sexual abuse, superficial nature of the music industry.

The Reflectors are also here to work outside the Penta, letting us know how things are going.

OVERALL, what we learn from the Penta.

One thing we learn is that no one is here to work alone. Projectors, you need the energy of the Generators, and Generators, you need the Projector to direct you, so you don't waste your energy spinning wheels working like a dog in the wrong direction. Manifestors, yes, you are the starters and can manifest what you want, but you need to have the Generators running your businesses and Projectors directing them. Reflectors, of course, cannot work without the support of the other Aura Types and provide wisdom and insight for us all.

This system shows us how to live and work together in perfect harmony (wow I just realized the lyrics to a Michael Jackson song, LOL). We are here to recognize the strengths of the other people we work with and support each other through the process of building things.

It also shows us: no one is better than another, and we all have strengths and weaknesses.

So Let's Put This Story Together for the Aura Types in Business.

Suppose we were working together to create a town center. The Manifestors would be the starters, and they would have the idea and start telling the town we are creating a new town center. They would get the money and start putting the plan into place. The Generators and Manifesting Generators would be those inspired and creative life forces to create the hall, bring in the colors, the design, the how to build it, the materials to build it, the energy to make it happen. The Projectors would be the ones who oversee, guide, and direct the project. Where it should go, who should do what for the fastest results, what should be built next, the order timeline, and direct the plan. The Reflector would know if this was the right place and thing the town needed for its next level of evolution. The Reflector, a significant key role for the project, would let us know if the project was suitable for the town, where the right location would be, and the project's health as it moved forward from idea to manifestation.

Each Aura Type has a role to play, and each person is the most fulfilled when playing their part. And yet, in our world today, most people are cluelessly conditioned to believe they are something they are not. They are told what to do, and no one takes the time to understand themselves before working like maniacs, hence the general chaos and pain in today's work environments. Obviously, this is a gross generalization. Conclusion: There are many cutting-edge leaders providing keen insight on these types of processes and awakening the zone of genius in their employees and helping to create inspirational environments. However, I would have to say these types of work environments are still in the rare minority.

So, of course, there are severe nuances with this, and everyone's chart is far more complicated than just their Aura Type, but this gives an overview of the roles.

Are you designed for solo ventures? We look at Instagram and Facebook ads and see many talented entrepreneurs with online programs or products containing systems for getting you to 7-figures. They tell you that you too can follow this logical system, and it will happen for you. It does, for about 5% of the people. Why?

We often say it is because the rest of the group did not implement, did not have a positive mindset, or didn't listen to the materials. There are so many reasons why you might have been told why that system did not work for you.

You probably took it on and made yourself feel like a failure. But here is a truth bomb, not everyone is designed for solo ventures. So, let's look at this in a new place in your chart.

Let's now look at the area in your chart that says:

DEFINITION. Pull out your chart, and in this area, you will see one of the words below, and I will explain how this will profoundly impact your dynamic in business. Maybe even making one of those high-end business offers obsolete for you. That means I may have just saved you 100k. WOOT!

Definition: This will be based on the Human Design Business model, not the consciousness awakened model. Meaning there are two ways to look at the Definition in your chart. For the sake of this topic of understanding business, we are discussing it in Human Design business terms only.

Single Definition: Those of you with this definition will feel a sense of being able to work alone.

Super comfortable being a self-starter, completing tasks by yourself, and capable of running your solo venture. There are a couple of factors to this, like if you are a Projector, you might need a Generator to give you the energy kick-starter in business, and if you are a Manifestor, you might need people for the day-to-day tasks.

However, the single definition is quick, they process information fast, and they can complete tasks alone. Great for SOLO VENTURES!

Split Definition: Here, you might see someone who has a little trouble getting things done alone. You work well in a partnership and might sometimes wonder if you are trying to do your own business. Why do I feel stuck?

This type of definition can be confusing because you are always looking for something to complete you and not in all the right places. In business, however, this definition might need a collaborative type of work environment, like the right business partner, mentor, or coach, to get the business momentum and juices rocking. This Definition will do amazingly well in partnerships or maybe even small businesses depending on the Penta Gates.

Triple Split Definition: This definition might work best in larger groups.

A small group or smaller partnership type of situation might feel suffocating or stifle your flow. You might enjoy groups of people that you can move in and out of.

Maybe, people you can connect with occasionally while working in different types of environments. You might wonder why you have blocks when trying to work alone or just with a partner. Explore how you can have more prominent groups to move in and out of, or if writing content, maybe go to a café or other place to write to be around other Auras. Suppose you are trying to do an entrepreneurial venture on your own. In that case, look around and notice with your Strategy and Inner Authority which outside influences might be able to support you if you feel overwhelmed, stuck, or confused with any aspects of your business.

Quadruple Split Definition: Since these Types are pretty fixed and process things at a slower pace, it is possible they may work well in solo ventures. However, if you are a Quad split, notice how you work with others. Are you open to change or suggestions? Also, for those of you who might have one of these Definitions on your team, you might be the one adjusting to them.

This may or may not be accessible depending on the partnership. These people have a super-fixed nature that needs to be honored, and nothing will change that. So, it is possible doing business alone might be better for them. Having people and other Auras coming in might assist, and going slow to learn new ideas. They must challenge themselves to learn and see things from new perspectives.

No Definition: Reflectors can work in solo environments sometimes; however, they are here to revitalize and lift up the energy of others. They can use their connoisseur valuations for businesses to answer: what should be different or what should remain the same? Every day for them, when operating correctly, will be unique. Again, these Types will do well by not having time pressures, learning their Design, and having the patience to wait in whatever career they are in. No Definition can work in solo ventures or small businesses if they have the right work environment. They might even enjoy larger companies. I have seen many thrive in solo entrepreneurial businesses.

Business Dynamics

There are many things to look at when considering business by design. The next interesting thing to analyze is when three people come together and form a Penta certain Gates and Channels in their chart metamorphose into business skills.

I know this sounds mystical but think of it like this.

At home, you have certain quality traits or skills you can rely on and are familiar with. But if you are anyone who has ever worked in a store, business, corporate office, you know that sometimes in these environments, certain aspects of your personality come to life that you didn't even know you had. Maybe in the office, you all of a sudden realize you are great at sales? Or perhaps you understand the numbers, the marketing, the spreadsheets with a fervor never before seen? This might happen in areas you weren't even professionally trained in before. This magical experience that I am sure most of you can relate to in some way is the powerful force of the Penta.

When the group comes together and forms this Trans-auric entity, what happens is specific skills come alive in the group.

There are two arms, two legs and a body of this Penta field. The arms reach out, the body stabilizes, and the legs walk the business to its proper destination. If one of these limbs is missing, you can imagine there might be an illness in the company. Suppose the business or group can utilize this intel to understand the business dynamics. In that case, it is like having business assessment tools, private coaching, family therapy all in one and all on healthy performance high-end enhancement drugs. (Do we have those out there?) It potentially will heighten the entire business group to all-new levels of awareness of how to work together, support the individual, and assist the final vision of the group to reach its destiny or financial goals with grace.

So, a Penta is an energy formed in this group dynamic. When you are alone, you are one type of person, yet you are another when you are in a group. Imagine a work environment or office you have been a part of in the past. Did the workplace have a vibe? Were you different when you were there? Did it take on a personality and a force of its own?

When I was in the corporate world, I worked for a born-again Christian company. They ran the place with fear. More specifically, the fear of losing your job.

Whenever they wanted to motivate the group, they would fire someone without warning, letting the bloodshed run through the office and instill the fear in us to work harder.

This kind of environment, even though there were amazing things about this company, was entrepreneurial in nature, based performance on results, not the hours put in, which was great for me. I even worked from home, so I wasn't technically even in the environment. It was all women, and I was serving the health and wellness of women in the world. I traveled to many exotic places living very well in unique hotels with fine meals. And yet, this FEAR became a part of me. I was conditioned by this fear.

I became almost anxiety stricken around losing my job, and I was paralyzed in fear. They made it seem our roles were coveted, and we should be super grateful to be there, and we would receive the ax with one wrong move. Now, of course, I can review my anxiety in terms of my Jewish family lineage or my persecution from Atlantis, or my own past trauma wounding around money. You can see this as a Projector panic of not feeling capable of supporting myself financially or keeping up in the Generator world. I am sure many other Projectors think this too. But, because of the conditioning element of the Penta, it trapped me. This anxiety began to dissolve when I entered different types of worlds where people knew they created their own reality and felt confident in who they were – an important note about the Penta.

This force of the company is a conditioning element. However, I do not consider myself religious at all and was not influenced by this mindset. I see myself as open to all religions; I understand the basis to be the same. I see all of humanity having the same energy force or God force. I am spiritual. Here I was not influenced by the dynamic, but I became one of them in the area of control by fear.

It was overwhelming; this fear slowed my leap into starting my own business. Eventually, I saw I was being "homogenized" by the force of the group Penta of the business tribe I was in while working – yes even from my home office.

Think back to any experiences you might have had with a company, business, group, office, job, or class environment where the collective energy created a force that influenced you.

Exercise

Look back at your history, and all of your jobs, companies, groups, businesses, networking groups, and contemplate these exercises:

Write out the themes that you experienced when you may have conformed to the group's energy in any past jobs, careers, or business environments you were associated with.

Contemplate if you were more comfortable in smaller businesses, 3-15 people, or large companies.

Which type of businesses did you shine in?

Do you feel you took on the energy of the business environment you were in? Was this positive or negative for you?

Did you enter into the career, job, business correctly based on your personal Strategy or Inner Authority?

The Penta Skills Alone or in a Group.

PULL OUT YOUR CHART, and let's take a look at you in a Penta!

There is only one area in the chart that the Penta will look at, it is the Channels from the Sacral to the G-Center and the G-Center up to the Throat. There is a total of 6 Channels and 6 Channels only, which is 12 Gates. If you don't have any of these Channels or Gates, it just means you might not self-actualize well in a small group. You might feel uncomfortable in a small business. Instead, you might thrive in a partnership, a larger group of 16, or in a solo venture. All of this is revealed in your chart. Yup, it can get that specific.

When you pop into a small group, you experience another dimension of who you are. This happens as well when you enter into a group of 16. This larger group dynamic is called a WA and we will cover this in a bit too!

Let's just say your Channels form a force inside you to either self-actualize or hit new levels of your potential in a smaller group, or you might feel drawn to the larger organization and even feel a need to lead. If you have one of these Channels within you, then you will notice the dynamic to lead a larger or smaller business depending on where these Gates are in your chart. I know, talk about an assessment tool! Imagine if you can assist your team in understanding how to best reach their potentials in the office.

Each Gate in your chart will have a special energy when you are alone or a business superpower when you are in a small group. Also, if a Gate is missing in the Penta there will be a gap or an illness that may appear in the business if any Gate of the Penta is not held by any of the members in the group.

So again, once you get to three people in a company, a Trans-auric entity is formed. Yes, the parts make up a force more significant than the individual, and this moving energy is the business company. So, within this Auric field, there is a way individuals can consciously understand how it operates and get the best performance out of it.

You can also understand that when you are wrapped up in the energy of the Penta, you can only grow, move, or evolve at the pace of the group.

So, imagine your family dynamic. If your family believes that there is no cure for cancer, this belief is deep-rooted in the Penta. This is the belief system that is integrated and conditions the Aura of this particular tribe. Once you are in motion with this Penta, you are conditioned by the force of the movement.

So, if this tribe believes that you cannot heal cancer and you are in this tribe, and you happen to get cancer, you are deeply conditioned and held to the standard of this belief system.

To move into a place where there is a possibility you might have to engage with a Penta that has a different belief system. You might need to move into a community with people who have healed cancer with their mind, uplifted frequency, and nutrition, which has often happened in many communities I am engaged in. This is possible within different tribes, now. Not to get too off-topic but read *The Journey* by Brandon Bays or Joe Dispenza, and you move into a different group mind or Penta field. So, if you want to heal cancer, you might want to involve yourself in a Penta force that will condition you or allow your energy to move or heal at the rate of a new mindset! The Penta force has power, and particularly right now, we are all being asked to reevaluate the values of our tribes, including our family tribe.

This also has to do with business. Suppose you are in a

business model that believes you need to suffer for results, that everyone has to put in 9-to-10-hour days to succeed, and this is not in alignment with what is right for you. In that case, you might need to remove yourself from the energy of that group for you to evolve to your next level.

Groups and businesses have a force field, and in Human Design, we see it and explain it here in the Penta. We will look at this by analyzing each of these Gates and how it operates when it is alone and then what happens when it joins up in a group. Just like you will begin to notice how you are different when you are in a group. How you morph and change and maybe even become more skilled in an area you were never trained in when you are called or recognized by the group to fulfill specific roles.

As we move into the Era of the Individual, it will be crucial that groups learn to recognize the power and the unique role each person in the group has to offer. Individuality and personalized gifts and skills will need to be identified. The days of sacrificing for the tribe are over. We will be encouraged to make our own decisions, take care of the individual needs first, and as a person is fully self-realized or actualized, the group can evolve together to the next level.

The Penta is made up of these Channels: The Channel 2-14, which is called The Beat. Channel 5-15 is called the Channel of Rhythm. The Channel 29-46 we call the Channel of Discovery. Channel 8-1 is referred to as the Channel of Inspiration. Channel 13-33 is called Channel of the Prodigal. Channel 7-31 is referred to as the Channel of the Alpha.

As we analyze these Channels in business, we see these traits coming out when these Gates and Channels are in a business environment. So, in other words, these are not the same definitions you will see in these Gates when you are looking at just Human Design alone. Each Gate operates differently when alone. Then when they are with a group of three or more people, here are the definitions of the Individual Gates. Gates running from the Sacral Center to the G-Center to the Throat. These Centers will be explained in detail in the following Chapters. These are the Gates of the Penta.

Gate 31: In the I Ching, this is called Influence. When you are alone, this is called the Gate of Democracy. When you enter a group, it awakens the skill to organize – knowing the energy of each individual in your office and what they can bring to the table, business, company, or team. Along with this is a natural ability to overlook the operations of any given organization.

Gate 8: In the I Ching this is known as Holding Together. When alone this is called the Gate of Contribution. The need to individually make a contribution to the world. In a business, we see this as natural skills to interact with the public. A PR specialist for how you get your company or product noticed. An essential key to business success, wouldn't you agree? How do people see your product, or what can you do creatively to make the public want your products?

Gate 33: In the I Ching this is Retreat. When alone this Gate is called Privacy, the secret keeper. When you are in a small group, this energy becomes the ability to oversee the process of the business dynamics. Comprehensive overview of the company and naturally understands how the past operated to form current success. Also, what you can do next by reviewing past successes and failures.

Gate 7: In the I Ching, this is called The Army, when alone this Gate is called Self in Interaction. When in business, this skill turns into seeing the future possibilities and planning for the upcoming needs of the company.

Gate 1: In the I Ching, this is known as The Creative, when alone this Gate is called Self-Expression. In business, this becomes the creative way to sell the product or services, which has to do with sales. You naturally have a way to tell people about the business, service, or product that will help with sales.

Gate 13: In the I Ching, this is The Fellowship of Man, alone this Gate is called The Listener. In business, we see an impressive natural ability to keep track of all the numbers. Accounting prowess even though you may not have been trained in this arena, but you might naturally have a way of tracking the numbers, which products are most profitable.

Gate 5: In the I Ching, this is Waiting, alone this Gate is called Patterns. In a small group or business, this becomes a reliable nature that can pull everyone into the Group, office, company together as a team. In a group, this turns into trustworthiness or reliability and routines we need for success.

Gate 2: In the I Ching, this is The Receptive, when alone this Gate is The Keeper of the Keys. When in a group, you might have the ability to see the company's view or vision and direction of the business. Natural power for the right timing for subsequent product launches, training, or moving forward or slowing down.

Gate 46: In the I Ching, this is Pushing Upward, alone this Gate is called Love of the Body. It is very different in a group dynamic. In a group, this is the Aura stabilizer, which makes everyone feel like they are one with the business group. People with this energy will make everyone in the group feel special, excited to be there, and long to be part of the community.

Gate 15: In the I Ching, this is called Modesty, alone this Gate is called Extremes. When in a group, it is the social behavior, customs, and inner life. This energy creates a positive feeling of connectedness with the group; it is a camaraderie of our created group dynamic – when absent many people in the company may not feel connected, committed, or loyal to the group.

Gate 14: In the I Ching this is the Possession in Great Measure; alone, this Gate is called Power Skills. In business, it becomes the foundation of resources or funding, money for the group – critical foundational piece for the company.

Gate 29: In the I Ching, this is The Abysmal, alone this Gate is called Perseverance. In a business, this dynamic brings with it allegiance or commitment, integrity, and loyalty of the Group. If you ever wonder why people might steal, cheat, or not want to commit to the vision of the company you might not see this energy in the Penta.

These Gates are found in the individual charts, but when you look at a business you want to make sure all of these assets are found within someone in the group. So, what you would want to do is run everyone's charts and make sure you find at least one person with one of the above-listed Gates in your business.

If you have a gap (meaning one of these skills is not found in someone in the group in their chart) in any of these areas, even if someone was trained in sales, if they don't have this energy in their chart, it just might feel like something is missing in the realm of sales. Like, wow, we have an incredibly trained team, but our averages are far worse than other businesses.

You might feel like we just can't compete with other sales teams; what are we doing wrong? It just might be the Aura Mechanics.

When you look at the charts of your individual members from an overall perspective, you see that each person has a part to play, and if something is missing, you must fill in the gaps. Now, the most important thing to learn about Penta energy is that it exists.

The second most important thing you need to learn is that when a business incorporates the mindset that the whole will succeed by honoring the individual, you will thrive.

The idea of this Penta is to understand how different each person is and try to allow their skills to shine. If you are trying to manufacture a business by putting these pieces together, you might also fail miserably, and this is working backward if you are trying to piece these Gates together.

You take the business you have, look at the charts to assist people in knowing themselves, honor the process of how they operate as in their Type, allow them to live their unique genius, and watch as pieces start to fall into place.

Just being aware can assist the change.

Again, actively trying to manufacture a business and piece it together with this intel doesn't necessarily create a successful business entity.

The reason for this, as you have read above, the very most important KEY in this intel, is that EACH and every person must honor their Inner Authority, which means you can't force anything to happen.

The Manifestor might be able to Innovate the movement forward on a project, but for everyone else, trying to initiate the Penta often goes against a person's truth and ends in failure. So, it kind of feels like a Catch-22 – yeah sort of, I know, and I'm sorry!

LOL.

Awareness is the sunshine to the acorn, the Strategy and Inner Authority is the water, so if you live your Design with this awareness, often the perfect Penta will be brought into place in your team without you forcing it or "making it happen."

So, the critical point here once again is AWARENESS. As you become aware of this stuff, you can notice what is happening within the energy of a given structure. Then you Respond and/ or Wait for the Invitation, and things will naturally unfold, and new powers will be drawn into the organization.

So, even with the Business STUFF – Following your Strategy and Inner Authority is STEP 1!

So, if you would like to know more about the specifics of how these dynamics operate, don't forget to grab the accompanying PDF for more juicy details.

Suppose you want to know why your business might not be making sales, who is best designed to be an administrator, who might naturally be the group's best accountant, who is the one who should do the heavy marketing, or who should reach out to the outside vendors. In that case, this might be your new tool. If you notice you have a lot of backstabbing in the group, or no camaraderie, all of these things can be shown and assisted by looking in at the group charts!

Entering Big Business – Drumroll Please!

Once you move into a larger organization, you speak in a group, you are involved with a team that is over 15 people – we then have an entirely new Aura emerge. This is called the WA.

Welcome to the wild ride of Human Design that just gets deeper and deeper. Here are some characteristics of the WA:

- The WA integrates Tribal and Individual Circuitry and energy.
- This entity or creative expression of more giant formations of people, meaning in events, companies, any group of people, something magical happens. There is a creative impulse, an ignition or spark of the Individual moving through the business arena within the world of the material plane and business leadership.
- This larger group is rooted in tribal culture, but it nurtures a unicorn's Individual expression.
- Whereas in the Penta, you are controlled within the Penta energy's constraints and do not honor a person's mutant expression. Yes, if you have a lot of Individual Circuitry, you may feel better in a larger group than a smaller one. No, you were not crazy for not being recognized!
- Channel 2-14 is the Channel that links both small and large businesses, it is connective energy, and it is the only Channel in both entities.
- It houses the energy and leads the way in the "haves" and the "have nots." In other words, part of the dilemma here is the deep questioning of how you will lead when you have, and others have not.

If you have one of these Channels or Gates, this is the energy of the WA. Now the WA is an exciting force; it will be more likely to honor the mutant expression, and we like this!

If you have noticed that maybe you feel stifled by smaller businesses, you thrive once you are given a leadership role in a larger company. Or this could also translate into leading groups, having speaking engagements, or even online organizations with more significant amounts of people. Each of these Channels operates differently if you are simply analyzing the Human Design information than when you are approaching this from the business perspective, so again keep that in mind.

Here are the six Channels of the Wa:

The Channel of Mutation 3-60 When simply analyzing, your Human Design is an intense Channel of Mutation. When in business, this is the CEO energy or natural leadership for innovation. We all know how important it is to innovate. If you don't keep up with the times, think Tower Records; you can be left dead in the water. Once these new musical digital formats came out, they had to be sharp enough with innovation to keep up with the times. I believe they did have an opportunity and tried to change but couldn't imagine people not wanting to go to the Tower Records store to thumb through the album covers as part of their music experience. That inability to innovate dinasaured (yes I made up that word) the entire company. News on the street is that Tower is trying to make a comeback, so my advice, hire someone with this Channel.

The Channel of the Beat 2-14 you will notice is in both the Penta and the WA. This is also known as the Lucky Money Channel. It is the body and foundation for a business, a super important Channel in both small and large companies. Here is what is interesting about this Channel. Often there is something to overcome around the energy of money with Individuals with this energy. In a more significant industry, this is the direction of finances, the flow of the investing, funding, and the timing of business transitions.

The Channel of Mating 59-6 and the Aura-busting sexual energy of this Channel has special power. But, when it comes to the more significant Industry and larger companies, this has to do with Investigation, research and development of the product or environment of the business.

The Channel of Preservation 50-27 is often referred to as the Channel of Values. This energy in larger businesses becomes the leader, nurturer and protector of the company. We see those with this Channel lead large groups and provide a sense of the tribal or group value, fierce feminine security, and leadership within the organization. They know what the future entails in that they are future-oriented forward thinkers with visions to direct the motion of the company and the employees.

The Channel of Shock 25-51 is an incredibly spiritual Channel when not in business. This is the Shamanic energy that initiates a shock to the entire tribe to live in an awakened, more powerfully connected way of life to the unseen forces of the Universe. When it comes to business, this is the leading edge of competition. This is the power that moves a company forward as a fierce competitor in the brand, marketplace, and product design doesn't matter in the area of business you are looking at. This energy will keep you on the leading edge of any competitive marketplace. Those with this energy will have a competitive spirit that they bring to the group often without even realizing others are competing with them. Others may feel intimated by this competition, and instead of being their best, they will try and smash the likes of leaders with this energy.

The Channel of Money 45-21 This is the Channel called The Money Line or the Channel of the King or Queen. This is leadership energy around money and is the spokesperson for the tribe.

This leader needs to put the values of the tribe over personal gain to be a good leader, which is true in business. This CEO energy is all about high valued management, leadership, and education. As a company leader, this energy must know they are only as strong as their weakest member. You awaken a powerful force forward when you serve not your gains but the team's overall strength. Through training and education, you can empower the team to self-actualize and grow, bringing forward the best possible production for the business.

With any of these Gates or Channels, you may understand that you might flower in a CEO type of role when in front of a larger group. You also might be called for your own businesses to grow or expand into larger organizations.

You can contemplate these business Channels by looking back on your past, how you felt in different environments, and exploring your current positions. As you gently reflect these influences in your career or any group you are involved in, you will naturally be led to flower in these new ways.

For me, I absolutely was not recognized as a Projector or an Individual in small groups. I have Penta Gates but no Channels. However, I have WA Channels and have always felt called to lead larger groups and organizations and thrived in Corporate when I was given more significant leadership roles for larger groups.

Also, learning about my business acumen and skill helped me overcome the stigma we Projectors get when we first come to Human Design.

We are seen as lazy complainers, which, yes, happens after years of not being recognized and getting bitter, but also as those who can't make anything happen in business, so it might be incredibly disempowering at first, when you learn your Design, as you are trying to hit your stride as a Projector. It is incredibly empowering to know you are here for business and to lead in the world of entrepreneurship, or anywhere in the business world, as long as you are recognized, you don't have to overwork, and you can lead, guide, and direct while also being just a little outside of the energetics of the business you are in. Meaning you take some alone time, maybe you can lead from home, work fewer hours, etc. However, you are here to work. Knowing your role in business is super helpful in the world of entrepreneurship, and also, as we move closer and closer to the year 2027 and the wheel begins to shift, all Types need to understand their proper roles in businesses.

So, this brings me to the topic of the upcoming mutation – 2027. Hold on, because this shizz is about to get SUPERSONIC interesting!

Chapter 10

There Is a Shift Coming in 2027 – The Revenge of the Mutant

The glue of the Cross of Planning as held together with our lives for the last 400 years is dismantling. But there will soon be no inherent need, drive, or purpose fulfilled through coming together to protect that way of life. This means we will basically end up with the breakdown in the way in which society is going to function.
Ra Uru Hu on the 2027 shift

Just to be clear, it will not be complete on January 1st, 2027. There is no one date, but a new global cycle is definitely happening, and it begins around 2027, but we are already seeing the shift now, and it will last another 411 years after 2027.

The last cycle we are moving from is the AGE OF PLANNING (called The Incarnation Cross of Planning). We are moving to the ERA OF THE INDIVIDUAL (The Incarnation Cross of the Sleeping Phoenix). I am going to break this down for you in a way that you can notice what happened over the last 400 years, why things are falling apart now, what is coming energetically in the future, and how you can peacefully navigate these rocky waters.

Once I break this down for you, the importance of living your Design will become even more imperative. Don't worry; I will dismantle this shift down in laypeople's terms and hopefully provide some simple, practical insight to help you navigate these times of great upheaval.

The first essential thing to understand is this global cycle is sort of like looking at the Aura Type for all of humanity. We are moving from one type of Circuitry that created the last 411 years to a radically different type of energy that will be holding the human Aura Mechanics together for the next 411-year cycle.

Understanding these changing times will help you realize why it is so essential to be operating as yourself, why you may have felt like a black sheep your whole life, why you might be feeling the call to this intel. Why, if you have a lot of Individual Circuitry in your chart, you might be here to lead the way in this shift. The other important point here is that many people will be confused, lost, scared, and seeking answers as we make this shift. Again, why it is essential to understand how these Aura Mechanics operate and why it is imperative to share this intel with the world. Understanding these shifts from this perspective will help us sit back and relax into the witness consciousness, step back, remove the proverbial "boogie monster" out there making things fall apart, and allow change to happen.

The Cross of Planning
1615-2026

Discerning these times is especially important when we look out onto the world and see how confusing things appear already. In 2020 what was vividly revealed was that there was no source of news, commentary, information that we could 100% safely rely upon. The narratives were so different, the facts were twisted from most sides, there were agendas, and we each had a differing way of interpreting what we heard. So, we couldn't agree on the same reality, and this is going to intensify as we move closer and closer to the shift of the wheel cycle according to Human Design knowledge.

This shift might be very disorienting for many people. When people are bewildered and scared, they don't think straight. The tool of Human Design, when downloaded, was said to be for these changing times. So, understanding the shift in the Aura Mechanics and your role during this shift is an incredibly invaluable tool.

Understanding the Astrological shift from the Human Design perspective reveals a global consciousness or one shared collective field for all of humanity. Or it can be referred to as the Human Epoch, the collective human Auric field. Some people may refer to it as the collective consciousness that impacts all of humanity and moves in 411-year cycles.

We have been in the Era of Planning ranging from 1615 to 2027. During this time of Planning, the Channels and energy were very much based primarily in Tribal Circuitry. The Tribal Circuitry means most of the global collective Epoch was held together by a Tribal rule we could all agree on. It was in our Auric field, and it kept things about the Collective and the Tribe in place. We had energy and rules around the way things should be done, and if you did not follow this rule, you were not accepted, nor would you thrive during these times. The Tribal Circuitry includes all things tribal-like, including family, corporations, companies, governments, universities, religious organizations, banks, capitalist structures, cults, any network or organizational group you have to belong to would all be considered Tribal systems. All of these things were built during this Cross of Planning, and we just assumed it was the way of the world. However, according to Human Design, it was simply the Aura Mechanics that were holding these energies in place.

Because of these Aura Mechanics, in the last 411 years, we witnessed many things come to pass, including our monetary and banking systems being created and developed. We saw that Capitalism was firmly established and strengthened along with the stock market, large companies and financial institutions gained extreme power. Big business was revered, school system curriculums established as fact, Government systems were built, Non-Profit Institutions, Health Care Systems, Insurance Systems, and all education was institutionalized from elementary to Ivy League schools. The general theme of these times was based on the bargains of the tribe. The primary Channel 40-37 is the Cross of Planning, the Channel of community bargains, which means what we will exchange for goods and how much this exchange will be worth, is all held in this Channel. The question here is, how to climb up the hierarchy, control power systems, and gain in both? The energy here was also that those who belonged to the tribe were loved, revered, and honored. Those outcasts who couldn't keep up, the homeless, the mentally impaired, etc., were cast out. The Tribal Circuitry theme is one of love and acceptance but if, and only if, you follow all of the rules of the tribe. Otherwise, it can be pretty aggressive, violent, vicious, and non-forgiving. All religious wars are fought in the name of my tribe is better or more important than your tribe.

Another theme of this energy is that it is far more critical that the tribe succeed than the Individual thrives. We have witnessed this play out in ways like the institutions demanding that their success is far more essential than individual employees' well-being. Think McDonald's and how the organization's wealth and success are more important than the grunt worker being able to afford a livable wage or the consumer being fed healthy life-sustaining food that will nourish them.

In this Cross of Planning era, we had themes bouncing back and forth of trusting authorities versus lack of trust in these same authorities. The theme of shifting between feeling aloneness and feeling the force of work being your entire focus. This notion would play out by people putting their careers first above human connection and finding themselves coming home alone after long hours in the office feeling very alone.

We also focused on talents and skills as the leading player in achievement and what we thought was the pinnacle of success. This focus on skill seems so crucial to our culture it is almost shocking we might shift out of it. It is hard to imagine we would ever find more value in human kindness, personal development, self-growth, compassion, and soul expansion compared to, let's say, entrepreneurial billionaire skills. However (thankfully), this is precisely where we are heading!

During this Era of Planning that began in 1615, it is

incredible to contemplate all that humanity built. We were Aura Mechanically fixed in the Tribal Circuitry, the country, family, and corporations, and these structures moved our values, focus, and communities forward for over 411 years. We built so much during this time. The United States became a world power, capitalism proliferated, highway grids were built, trains, airplane travel, automobiles, suburbs, malls, online stores, so much was produced. Giant company lobbyists with their systems of power were established deep into the foundation of how things operated. Those people with the most outstanding skills and most impressive talents were the people who rose to the top during this era. We were all indoctrinated or conditioned to have faith in corporations, 401ks and to follow the American Dream. (Of course, other countries understand this concept as well.) Tribal guidelines for a life were expected to be followed. We were told to give over our individual lives for country, family, to raise the children, for the good of the industry, or for the corporations we worked for. We were taught to work hard for the organizations, surrender to the paycheck, and take care of family responsibilities. It was deemed selfish if we didn't want to bend over backward for our tribe or the family. We were outcast as black sheep or ostracized if we got divorced, didn't want children, or didn't have the skill to rise up the ranks in corporations or industries. Well, anyone who did not follow the system was seen as a rebel, subversive, or outcast. Independent thinking was not applauded. Individuals were not acknowledged for their inner achievement or personal growth; very few people honored or even saw any value in it.

Most of society was trained to take on the religion of their parents, not to think for themselves or to find their own relationship with God. The religious institutions gained power and prestige over the last cycle. As we move closer and closer to 2027, we are already seeing their fall, as the Aura Mechanics lose the grip, control, manipulation, and greed being revealed.

And society has begun to lose its faith in these institutions, and it was shown how damaging and destructive fundamentalism could be within all religions.

Many of the universities lost their clout as they stopped progressively supporting the cutting edge of science and fell into small-minded institutionalized education that only focused on the values of the tribes and corporations. The universities trained students to become workers to fall into line rather than individuals to discover their unique understandings of the world. The school systems became outdated, and this is witnessed with the loan debt and the inability for many graduates to become employed as the Aura Mechanics lose their glue.

As we can see, all these structures we have built are slowly losing our respect, and these institutions will continue to slowly dismantle as the Aura Mechanics will not be held in place any longer to support their development.

We see signs of this transition as the mechanics from the Cross of Planning holding these industries in place are already beginning to fall away.

Signs of this change:

- Mistrust of the Government.
- Disillusionment of the corporate model.
- People losing pensions and retirement.
- Distrust of the banking industry.
- People taking their health into their own hands (losing faith in the medical institutions).
- Much of the cutting edge in science and healing is on the outskirts. (Science not keeping up because focused on the $$ rather than true innovation.)
- Universities are increasing the student loan debt creating a culture of debt (this might get adjusted), but the education system is still falling behind.
- Parents pulling children out of public schools for lack of

trust of the system/education.

- Political systems are acting out with more propaganda/corruption and losing the faith of their people.
- The priests and gurus are being taken from their throne. (People going direct to connection w/God.)
- Fake News: we don't know what facts to trust as significant news stations are losing clout.
- Independent news is beginning to get more downloads, views, credibility than traditional news sources.
- New ways to handle money, including cryptocurrency systems rather than traditional banking.
- Family structures redefining the traditional model.
- Family values questioned, traditional family roles questioned.

People are becoming disillusioned in many of these areas already.

Not too long ago, finding a career and doing the same thing with the same company for your lifetime, then saving for retirement, was expected.

There are many examples of people sacrificing the self for the government, the country, the tribe, the family. You see this in business a lot, people sacrificing their health for their careers. This type of thinking will become outdated, but for now, as it is losing its grip, the old structure is grasping at straws for control to maintain power.

As we move into the Era of the Individual, we will be moving into a time of human awakening, understanding self on a deep level. Individuals will realize that the one-size-fits-all life model just doesn't work anymore. Infrastructures of the large industries, the governments, corporations, hospitals, religions are all losing their power. Individuals will take their care into their own hands, and they will rely on themselves to find ways to make money and heal themselves. The focus is on the unique individual self-expression, self-actualization, self-empowerment, the breakdown of barriers and façades in order to genuinely bond with one another. So, just with that introduction, you can feel how different this subsequent shifting of the wheel will be. So, let's get into it, shall we!

The Emerging of the Era of Individual (the Cross of the Sleeping Phoenix) 2027-2438

The Era of the Individual has an entirely different power dynamic than what we have experienced since the 1600s. As we move closer to this time, we are beginning to feel the transformation approach. You might even say, if you looked out into the collective culture, you could see the shakedown happening now.

As we mentioned, there will be a slow breakdown of bigger rooted establishments in the new Era of the Individual, but this is just the beginning. What is emerging is instead of trusting the institution, we will be counting on the unique soul, integrity, the inner development of the individual. What this means is instead of putting our power into the hands of a force out-there, the individual will empower themselves as the authority of their own life. This individual success will not be based on what individuals have gained or accomplished, not based on their skills, the movies they have been in, or the athletics they strive in, no. The new accolades will be founded on the inner development of each person. Including all of the less valued outcomes like inner peace, kindness, compassion, stillness, integrity, to name a few. Right now, we don't have a clue how to recognize this in ourselves, let alone another person. We don't have an inkling how to spot this because the Aura Mechanics are not available yet. Of course, those fringe-dwelling individuals are like, this chick is singing my song! However, as the Aura Mechanics begin to move into place, we will develop the eyes to witness this level of development, honor it, strive for it. We will also notice these principles become the foundation of humanity's value systems. Of course, this new stage will be another 411 cycle, so how far along we will get in our lifetimes it's a crapshoot.

But, we will begin to notice the abundance of spirit and the honoring of uniqueness rather than the desire to follow the cookie-cutter model of life. Trusting our own unique individual expression instead of fitting into a group will slowly become the only way to feel comfortable. Busting down the inner barricades to connect at the heart and soul level with another person will be more important than rushing to expand the bottom line. The new cycle of the Individual Era is honoring the person over the tribe, country, organization, and even over the beloved institution of the family. Can you even imagine? We will long for personal development rather than the white picket fence, yard, two-car garage, children, dog, big house, etc. We will look up to those who have developed themselves inwardly rather than outwardly or materialistically. I am not saying people won't have both. I am saying we will not value material success over the fulfillment of personal growth, and we will not sacrifice the self to achieve material wealth. So many things we know today have this theme: marrying for money over love, betraying others to win, taking harmful substances to beat out the competition, kicking the little guy to make more money, greed, corruption ruling decision-making, I mean really the list could go on and on. Soon, we as a culture will far less often choose the ends over the means. We will develop awareness for this and desire the fulfillment of self above all else. It is a shocking awareness; it might shatter some of you to the core. Some of you black sheep out there – or we call those outcasts the ones in the family/tribe that can see through all the bullshit – are thinking, OMG, my time is almost here!

Some of the things we might experience as we move towards 2027 and beyond during the Era of the Individual:

- People will not be able to look to outside sources for any answers (if they do, they will experience confusion). This includes teachers, gurus, parents, psychics, leaders, presidents, government offices, coaches – all direct answers will be from inside.
- The only decision will be the one that is right for you from your own Inner Authority.
- Radical self-expression.
- The days of sacrificing the SELF for the tribe will be ending.
- In this Era, people will acknowledge the strength of the tribe is built when the Individual cares for the self-first.
- Self-actualization will be a primary goal.
- People will need support in understanding what makes them unique and learning how to express it.
- We will honor deep human connection rather than gaining riches.
- Spiritual awakening becomes essential.
- Independent thought, choice, and decisions will be honored.
- We will respect inside integrity rather than just the talent (jaw drop).
- People will want to have careers/jobs/businesses based on individual creative fulfillment.
- Spiritual connection to God will be personal, not through the church/rabbi/priest or anyone claiming to be the go-between.
- Fundamental self-reliance in money, food, health will become a priority.
- Knowing will be in the moment, and the king of logic as the only truth will be outdated. (This is a complex concept that I will go into more depth about in later chapters. Just know it is friggin cool, especially for those of you who are empaths, clairvoyants, or who just know

shit intuitively!)
- Radical Self-Reliance. (OK, I stole this term from Burning Man.)

Here is a recap on what this all might mean come 2027. Just because you are talented at making money, basketball, acting, and computer programing – if you are not a good person, you will hold less value in society, PERIOD. I am having another one of those moments when I want to connect with you all in the multidimensional time/space dimension whenever and whoever is reading this now – Let's all just take a breath in here; this is friggin HUMONGOUS.

If you are a person who self-actualizes, knows who you are, grows on the inside, is kind, and an aware, service-driven individual, you will be revered. WOW, what a concept.

In other words, we will care for the uniqueness of the Individual; yes, everyone is unique. We will honor the needs of each person and not stomp on the weak for the gain of the tribal ruler.

In the Era of the Individual, we are moving into a time of need for individuation. These times will force you into an arena where you might suffer if you don't understand your uniqueness. During these years, we will need NOT ONLY to know ourselves, live as ourselves but (and this is the hard part for many) allow others to live as themselves. We will be collectively releasing the control, the power, the manipulation of the herd mentality. We will see that the individual must learn how to become radically responsible for what they are creating and their own needs during this time. The shift will move from giving your power to a company, job, or government to personal power, inner contemplation, and the power inherent in focusing on the abundance of inner spirit. There will be a desire to break through the walls of separation to connect on a more authentic level with each other.

As we awaken the Era of the Individual, you must never abdicate control or decision-making to anyone outside of yourself. Being able to discover and honor other people's distinctiveness will be imperative, and you must learn how each person operates best and give them the freedom to operate as themselves. In other words, the common practice of manipulation through guilt, shame, fear will have much less power to impact and control people.

This is a massive shift. We will move away from prominent organizations and government structures taking care of us and into the power of the self-sufficient individual to take their life and power into their own hands. People will discover more and more unique ways to live, to create income, to become self-sufficient. You see this now with so many people living sustainably, buying up land, creating new lifestyles off the grid, tiny homes, van life, etc.

However, you might also see many people feeling lost or confused during this time. They might not understand how to make logical sense of what they are seeing or hearing, and because they are so used to seeking guidance from others rather than from within, they may become perplexed. Also, we might see many people seeking more than just a paycheck but not knowing exactly which way to turn or direction to take to achieve this goal. People might feel a deep need to take action towards a career, business, life that is not only deeply enjoyable and satisfying but allows the individual time, space, freedom to enjoy life. IMAGINE THAT!

According to this knowledge, Human Design, the wave or radical alignment to self, is the trajectory approaching us. I am sure most of you can see and feel this already coming. Each one of us will be asked if we are willing to take responsibility for our own lives, uniqueness, and personal mission here on the planet. No one will be able to come to the rescue anymore, but the flip side of this is also true; there is no boogie man out there taking power from you either. Meaning you have actively given over your power, and now is the time to take that power back. You will be endeared to awaken your inner strength, like no other time in history. However, if you choose not to, you will suffer more vehemently than any other historical period.

So, as you can see, this intel is a significant piece of information that can assist humanity in understanding this wheel change and in getting up on the surfboard, riding the wave, rather than letting it crush you to smithereens. OK, I am being overly dramatic, but am I? This insight from the Human Design map can assist us in these changing times drastically. It will give each person the buoy to navigate the rocky seas. It will provide a beacon of light during times of confusion about the things we relied on in the past losing their strength. You will only be able to turn to your own IA, which is literally the only way to navigate this shift.

The most important takeaway as we view these global cycles is that change is happening, and the only way through the confusion is to follow your uniqueness. Learn your strategy well, separate from what others have told you to do or to be, and live as your unique, vibrant genius!!

For those of you familiar with Human Design, you may have heard that the coming mutation of 2027 brings doom and gloom with it. You might be happy to know I don't see this. From my perspective, if you study the Aura Mechanics, you know that with each Gate, you have a shadow to it, a gift to it, or you have the highest expression available. So, when you look at the Gates and the Channels we are shifting out of and the ones that we are moving towards, it is true you can look at the lowest possible outcome to that shift, survival, or you can see the highest expression, spiritual awakening. So, you can see I have a different interpretation of the shift than many traditional Human Design perspectives. My unique view might have to do with my Innocence Motivation and Gate 25, allowing me to always see the highest potential in situations. (Of course, Ra had this Channel as well, but he had Desire Motivation, three Left pointing arrows leaving him focusing on the dissolving of the past, plus a little nihilistic.) In any case, I do believe there is a significant value in seeing this most elevated perspective right now as we are trying to decode what is happening in the collective and within us as we go through these changes. If you are like me, you do believe our thoughts are prayers and hold power. If you read about epigenetics or *The Biology of Belief* by Bruce Lipton, you will know that significant change comes with great opportunity. As we change, what we hold in our highest vision has the power and importance to create.

As I take this wheel shift one step deeper, meaning the above analysis was a general brushstroke, I am going to go a little deeper into the details. Before I do, the general idea is that each Incarnation Cross is shifting from one Gate to another. The shift is held together by one Gate we call the Lock Gate, representing a general theme throughout time. The Lock Gate does not change. If you want more on this again, check the accompanying PDF: https://foxy5d.com/pages/are-you-a-mutant.

I will be listing a couple of specific Gates here that we are shifting out of and moving into (not all of them, just a few that I found particularly relevant). The founder of Human Design painted a rather stark picture of this prophecy, but you have to understand these are energy dynamics. Now, of course, no one knows for sure what will happen as these energies shift.

But the Ra Uru Hu Human Design perspectives have a lot of people's heads spinning. Look around, add an end of the world scenario by a system that you wholeheartedly have come to trust implicitly (HD knows you better than you or anyone has ever known you), and see the fear saucers take over the eyes of those watching. This is why I want to point out quickly before I dive in entirely to the energetics of this mutation that we are moving away from Gate 42, the Gate of Finishing Things;

this was indeed the Plan (the Plan is the energy of the Lock) to finish things. What I mean by moving away is the wheel is shifting from this Gate as part of the collective Aura. The energy that held the collective Aura Mechanics in place will lift and shift in this new dynamic to Gate 51. So the Plan we have been in was flavored by the theme, ending things; now the Plan will be catapulting revelation to awaken higher wisdom. We can read the subtle energies of these shifts by understanding how these Gates operate. So, of course, there is a pressure to finish things, to have the end of the world, the rapture, the Armageddon scenario, or the Zombie apocalypse take over your consciousness. Why these themes are so prevalent in our world right now. This is the END from the Gate 42. Like I said, from the Gate 42, we are moving to the Gate 51, which is, you guessed it, SHOCK. So, we are finishing things, but it is not the end; it is the shock to a new enlightenment. The shocking shift from one dynamic to another. The surprise might seem like horror to some or transformation to another. The Gate 51 is also part of the spiritual awakening set forth by the Shaman of the tribe, the one who will shock you (or life) that will force you to your own spiritual development. We all know that substantial inner shifts usually come from big outer catastrophes or simply changing situations. Sometimes it takes a seemingly outside dark force or cataclysmic crisis to open our eyes and shock us into reclaiming our power back.

So, I want to come at this from a different perspective, one that establishes the foundation that we are frequency first. When we move into Alpha and Gamma brain waves, the foundation is that we change the body from being primarily matter to light. In the same way we melt an ice cube, we have control of our temperature to shift our perspectives. This is science now; it has been tested, tried, and found to be true (science is still essential now, but come 2027, the entire need for collective logic and the scientific experiment will be less valued). The reliance on logic or on science for every answer in the future will have less relevance. Even now, as we know, there are many things science has not yet discovered or been able to prove, but it is a solid foundation people still trust and rely on. The science foundation I am building on is, when we align to higher vibrational thought, we change the world we experience. One of the leaders in capturing the science of how this operates is Dr. Joe Dispenza; if you want to investigate this proven science, he has done a profound amount of research in this area.

When there is a shift of higher vibrational thought like moving to kind loving thoughts away from fearful anxiety-driven thoughts, we can awaken to more aligned, peaceful, kind, and loving people. More importantly, our literal body chemistry changes. We know that anxiety and stress cause so much dysfunction in the body that can be linked to many major illnesses. If we look to spiritual teachers and leaders rather than our propaganda, agenda-driven greed-driven leaders, we can witness when someone is self-actualized, they become better people. Of course, some teachers abuse this, and all of this is also coming into the light. However, it doesn't negate that many aligned and awakened leaders live and practice this stuff, and have become breathing examples of extraordinary lives. In this awakened state, for lack of a better term, people are driven to heal others, serve, see the best in others, and want the best for the highest good of all humanity, as opposed to seeking greed tactics for personal gain that harms another. Seeing people live a life without an ulterior motive is so shocking it is hard to absorb. There is so much corruption in our leadership, those who make the most money and basically run our country, that we can't imagine people honestly aligning to serve others humbly and authentically. So many of our leaders today are what I would deem somewhat sociopathic in their ability to put money first, win first, and get ahead first over the well-being of not only the people they serve but also their friends, employees, etc.

So, with this said, we have a stake in how we view these changing times, and we have a choice. We can grow, change, align to a high-vibe frequency, and create a positive outcome. Or we can hone in on the fear, the greed, the survival scenario and begin to manifest less than the opulent situation for ourselves and humanity as a collective. We are co-creating with divine energy, at the risk of sounding super woo (but I am already out of the woo closet, so deal with it!).

Meaning as we contemplate the upcoming changes on the planet, we must lean into the knowing that our thoughts, focus, and intentions play into the reality we will awaken into. And in my humble opinion, you don't need to change anyone's mind or care what anyone else believes because various parallel realities will begin to form around each person's frequency level. So, we are all free to view the world in our own unique way. I am simply laying out a possible reason for choosing the high road. The choice is yours and yours alone.

This is not such a crazy thought; ultimately, we have many different realities right now. Compare someone in jail to a multibillionaire living in a mansion on the beach. Don't you think these are pretty different realities living right here in the same world?

With all of that said, as we move from the Cross of Planning to the Cross of the Sleeping Phoenix, we can analyze this change from the detriment or the exaltation of each Gate. That is like saying let's look at a person's shadow aspects or let's look at a person in their highest exalted potential state. It matters how we view it; not only does it affect the outcome, but how we view this affects our present moment. How we view another person not only affects and brings out the best in the other person, but it also affects our OWN inner world NOW. NOW. The point is when we undergo this shifting view and align to the highest possible perspective, it serves humanity and our own personal frequency right here and right now. So let's get into the groovy highest expression of the coming times.

As I explore some of the energies of the specific Gates, it is essential to note that there are two shifts that will be happening when you go a little deeper into the 2027 information. Not only do we move from the Cross of Planning to the Cross of the Sleeping Phoenix, but there is a second wheel shift from the Cross of Maya to the Cross of Penetration. This is talked about much less, and I am simply going to mention a few of the changes, not all.

So here are some choices on how to view the coming 2027 shift and mutation on the planet. We are moving from the Gate 16 Skills to the Gate 20, the Gate of Metamorphosis, and starting in Line 6, which is wisdom. Over time, the lines move backward within each Gate from the Line 6 to the Line 1.

So, let me break this down for you. Instead of putting skill up on a pedestal – OMG you are a famous _____ (fill in the blank), we love you, we don't care you are evil or a rapist or pedophile, you say you didn't do it, please go make another album or movie. We will instead see your SKILL. You are smart, you are talented, but you can't be a monster and get away with it any longer. Just look at Harvey Weinstein and R. Kelly and how long they got away with the atrocious behavior that their entire entourage was aware of and covered up. You see now how we are finally beginning the process of breaking this down to where it belongs. We are finally holding people accountable for their horrendous behaviors and not letting them get away with wrong actions because of being skilled in areas that made them famous or rich. True honor belongs in the person who you are BEING, your wisdom, values, heart, NOT your skill. Your self-actualizing and if you are a good person are what we are going to care about in the future. Not how big your house is, or your TV deal... Those days are over (or soon to be over completely, well might take a couple of hundred years still, but we are getting closer). Skills will no longer be valued; they will be replaced with a moral fabric or personal development and empowerment not just to speak your truth but TO BE THE EMPOWERMENT, to be the truth. As we view the highest expression of empowerment and awakening the leadership of the self, we honor the best in others, who they are as a person and not their skill. This is one of the Aura Mechanics shifts humanity will experience from the changing of SKILL to BEING EMPOWERED. We can begin to awaken the highest expression of this Gate 20, empowerment in the NOW.

Moving from the Gate 37 Tribal Gate of Friendship (which ultimately has more to do with the bargains of the family and tribe) to the Individual Gate 55 of Spirit, and I love this one! We are transitioning from the family to individual spiritual, emotional expression. That means everything we have done for the last four hundred years is put the family structure first. You are born to get married, raise kids, and have a family. If you don't, even today in 2022, you are looked at as a bit of an outsider. I am an Individual and a Projector who has never really fit into this mode, many people still see me as a sort of rebel for this choice. For the most part, we are still viewed as freakish and pressured to live a "normal" life with kids and marriage. We are taught to raise those kids to go to college, force them to be driven and successful in the world, and to put family first. The family structure is what we strive for, what we believe in, the only people we truly trust. The family are the only people we are here to serve, to leave money to, to invest in. Our family is the moral fabric, THE WAY of the world, and this is all changing.

We are moving into the awakening of Individual spiritual abundance; yes, there is the chance for selfishness here. But, selfish according to whom? Primarily, only according to Tribal law is the Individual selfish. Think about this world we have been living in. Anyone in the family who disobeys the paternal rule or family tribal values is "self-seeking." If you don't want to go to the family reunion, or follow the family religion, take up the family business, you are the black sheep. If you break out from the moral fabric set up by your family, at the very least, you are seen as "self-centered." At the worst, you might be disowned or excommunicated from the tribe. Those awakening and choosing a unique path suitable for themselves as the Individual have in the past been deemed as "selfish" but soon will be honored for this choice. As this shift happens on the planet, more and more people will feel emblazoned to follow their unique path of inner riches, which will be respected. You may feel the need to awaken and spiritually express yourself, find abundance, true wealth not based on what your family wants you to do or what they think is suitable for you; but based on what is CORRECT FOR YOU BASED ON STRATEGY AND INNER AUTHORITY. WOOHOO, this is to be honored by the collective epoch... finally!

All we have been discussing will be The Way (the Lock keynote). This Way will replace the family as the Way we have been. Right now, before we shift in 2027, we are in 37.1; this can be seen as an intense Tribal Sensitivity. So this 37.1 is at its peak right now, before it shifts. How this would show up is each side (whatever side we are referring to regarding any issue) is feeling a heightened sensitivity to their tribal attachment. This sensitivity creates a faction and division, people firmly planting their feet in the belief MY VIEW IS THE BEST AND ONLY VIEW type of thinking. Thankfully we are moving away from this division soon. As you look around, you can witness how painful it is when everyone fights for their side with heightened sensitivity trying to protect the dying tribal value they created self-identity around. The pinnacle of this is upon us; people are holding on with dear fright to their tribe, whichever tribe this may be. They will do what they can to fight for their group, family, religion to be great again when they know that their tribal ideology is quickly becoming outdated. We are moving into the spiritual insight (spiritually, we are ALL ONE FAMILY, all the same frequency and energy, we are the ONE human race). So, my humble suggestion is, try to get involved with this change; being open to seeing things in new ways will make your life so much easier. You may want to get hip to this because this is the new Way.

So, jump on board; this Way will soon be THE ONLY WAY.

The personal individual spiritual expression will be the way in which humanity finds everything they used to find within their families, including values, purpose, the richness of life, meaning, commitment, and the direction to grow.

It matters how you hold this. If you can perceive spiritual awakening as being a personal inside job of the most high, of the greatest gift you can give the whole, as the most divine significant leap you can make, as opposed to seeing it as "selfish," then it might make it easier. If you want to survive the changing of the times and co-create its beauty, you will realize self-actualizing your highest, most authentic, truthful healed self just might be the greatest gift you can give to all of humanity.

So, again, we will be completing things. Yes, we are; we are finishing up many loose ends here. Looking back over the last 411 years, everyone has an end of the world scenario. We had the new millennium crash to the system, 2012 Mayan calendar ending, even the Human Design prophecy by RA (which is not current, BTW, because RA now transitioned many years ago) had pressure to finish things. This is because we are moving OUT of the Gate of endings. But our leadership (THE LOCK Gate 7 of leadership is shifting from Gate 62, the Gate of Details to the Gate 53, the Gate of Beginnings). So the leadership is innovating and moving into NEW BEGINNINGS! That means our new leaders will have the Aura Mechanics to see things in a new way. And look around, people, with all the friggin leaders now, wouldn't it be nice just to have them finish things and let an entirely new form of leadership emerge? It might not happen immediately or the way you may be envisioning right now. Remember, we are still a couple of years out from the new 411-year cycle to begin. So, right now, we are just seeing the breakdown of the old – all the systems showing the truth of their ugly systemic issues on BOTH sides. The truth is emerging, and as it does, new thoughtful leadership will begin to emerge. It might not happen in the way we think. We might not see new Founding Fathers take over Government. But those humbly leading from their homes, their private businesses in integrity and silently leading others rather than needing the prestige, power, fame, money which may lead to corruption (as we have seen far too often). You might even say that those in "leadership" positions are enslaved by their own greed and not leading us at all. So, this new leadership might just show up in people and in ways never before imagined. Just a contemplation. What we can say is that certain things are ending, there will be shocking new beginnings as the Gate 42 in the Plan moves to the Gate 51, and the new beginnings are happening in the way of new leadership. So, we might just be seeing the breakdown of the leadership we once respected into a band of organized criminals. Still, we can rest assured that something shockingly new is awakening within the new Aura Mechanics. So, it might be a wild ride.

We are moving from Gate 9, Focus, The Taming Power of the Small, to Gate 34, the Gate of Power. This shift is about moving out of focusing on tiny details (think of all the things in our world that need focus on small pieces from iPhone to taxes) – and into the personal individual power. Think for a moment the incredible amount of detail it takes to do what we have done in the last 411 years. Creating the banking system, capitalism, schools, hospitals, then, of course, the massive movement of computers, the Internet, just think for one moment the enormous number of details it takes just to make one of your favorite Netflix binge-worthy shows. The components built everything, we have thrived in the details, and this again is being replaced with a personal individual expression of power, empowerment, and, yes, some personal busyness. The personal drive will need to be in response; if people initiate and force the new transformation to happen, we will just be in a cluster-F of frustration. Gate 34 thrives when it is in response to the world around us, not making anything happen. So, thankfully the JUST DO IT motto may finally fall off the billboards. Don't cheer me; it is just the Aura Mechanics at work!

One great example of this Individual process is the career of Russell Brand. He has the Channel 34-20, was one of the first public famous people to outwardly admit fame and success does not come with inner riches. Not many famous people will admit this because part of the allure of this kind of success is being better than the crowd, getting off on the jealousy, and needing to be above the herd. I love listening to Russell Brand take down this pedestal of the superficial fame structure and instill values of inner development, new levels of healing, awakening, understanding who we are. He is a living, breathing example of awakening the Individual.

We are moving from a Collective Logical process that takes time and science to prove something as truth over time, to an Individual process of knowing truth in an instantaneous moment. Think about that for a second; the logical approach is breaking down and moving towards the Individual way of knowing. This means that society will respect a direct Individual knowing more than relying on science. How could this even come about? Well, if you have read any of the books of Donald Hoffman, you may realize that everything we have come to know in Time and Space is more like the inside of a *Grand Theft Auto* video game than the TRUTH of our reality. So, if there is a breakdown of reality as we have come to know it to be, a dismantling of the science we grew up thinking was truth? In that case, people might turn to masters or mystics who have explained the truth of reality for many centuries. These masters would usually point to each person and say, you have the truth within you. The seeking within will be the search, not for science to prove anything. I am not saying I know exactly how this will come about. I am simply stating that as the Aura Mechanics shift, how we understand the world will change.

The Individual way of understanding is like this: "I don't know, I don't know, I'm stuck, and then BOOM I KNOW! I don't know how I know. I just have a knowing or an insight." This is what we will respect, what we will need to personally experience before we simply take the word of the collective for our truth. The individual expression of knowing will have power and have validity in a way it never did in the last cycle. Over time, the details and logic, as the only things relied on for proof and knowledge, will loosen their grip and power on us collectively. This is amazing for those Individuals that JUST KNOW, and the collective logic has not recognized their knowledge as having any value. What a dramatically radical shift of perception. We are seeing this now with confusion on social media and fake news; no one knows what is going on or what to believe because logic is out the door. Not many people have been trained to trust, rely on or even look within for their individual knowing.

Another fascinating point is that there will be minimal Collective LOGIC Circuitry (in the two Crosses we are moving into, there will be one Gate) in our Aura Mechanics as we make this shift. The Collective Logic in the last cycle had an incredible amount of force or a lot of Aura Mechanics energy that held humanity together. The Logic Circuitry is the process of understanding reality through scientific experiments. Testing knowledge over time and making sure that things fit together logically for us to believe in them. This logic process held a large part of humanity's understanding of the world. Well, this entire system will have nothing holding it together. It is even hard to fathom a world without logic; the most essential thing humanity has rested its hat on in the past. All of humanity had this philosophy: "We can rely on this because it is science, it is proven, it makes sense." Well, of course, not all of humanity. There were always those who stayed committed to God's religious stories above science; you get my point. But now we realize this hard proven science fact has come to expose itself as a biased system, as much "belief" as religion. The Big Bang is not one hundred percent proven, yet logically along with Darwin and his scientifically proven method of evolution, we have come to develop all of this as fact. We teach it in our schools as though there is no other possibility. There might be a missing link, but if it doesn't fit with the logic, we just ignore it. We have been afraid of not knowing or uncertainty. We have used scientific facts to rule the world. Of course, much of what we came to know as fact has been disproven over the years. But to have the entire system of logic begin to dismantle might just throw much of humanity into a tailspin. The logical system will have no more glue, as Ra stated. One can only imagine how confusing this might be for many people. However, it will also be incredibly liberating and open the doors to an entirely new and more powerful way to view the world.

In the book *The Case Against Reality*, Donald Hoffman points out that once we can see beyond time and space, we will literally open the door to possibilities we cannot even fathom. He compares it to the video game mentioned earlier, *Grand Theft Auto*, when we finally realize that we are playing a game and we are more than our avatar. We will have the ability to go beyond the game and revolutionize the actual programming of the game. Again, a notion mystics have come to understand for centuries, but of course, the spiritual can't always be proven by science. It might appear that without the Aura Mechanics of logic keeping us stuck on one position of facts, we can open the door to the infinite possibilities our potential realities can offer us. Of course, this is simply my opinion of life without logic. So, no one knows what might happen when we no longer rely on logic, but I think we can all agree it is going to be super interesting to witness – grabbing my white cheddar popcorn now.

There is more. There is so much more coming in 2027. We are moving into an entirely new sexual expression that we see already. Homogenized sexuality is dismantling from society and the family's grip. There is a wholly new way to show homage and worship to sex, love, and family. At one time, we worshipped the family and tribal agreements, and now we will honor intimacy. The intimacy will not necessarily be defined by the family tribal rules. Each person will probably long to express themselves sexually in the family differently. With different types of marriages, same-sex, transgender, Asexual, Pansexual, just to name a few. Of course, we see this already happening and beginning its new world expression. We are moving from the Gate 40, the Gate of Loneliness, to the Gate 59 Intimacy. This Gate will be one of the few Tribal Gates in this changing Aura Mechanics. Meaning the family will not define the sexual agreements or dynamics of our relationships. Marriage may go out of style, so to speak, the traditional male-female roles will continue to be threatened, and we are already seeing this as the younger generations are redefining all of our pronouns and sexual definitions. The difference is now we can understand this as part of the Aura Mechanics shifting.

There are other changes in this upcoming global cycle shift (these were a few key themes), but the point here is how you hold things within your psyche now has POWER. How you choose to see the unraveling, the collective breakdown will impact not just YOU NOW but your future... So focus wisely. As we can learn and practice to sit back in the passenger consciousness and watch the wheels go by, we can be a more neutral observer to these fantastic shifts. No one knows exactly how this world will look as the breakdowns begin; there may be many holding on to authoritarian control. However, your inner world cannot be controlled, and this is the one true freedom you will always have.

The simple answer is that we can rely on one thing as we move through these changes. Not the news, the government, not the leaders or the gurus, not the Internet, or influencers' ideas, not even the Gods you have come to trust. The only thing you can rely on 100% during these times is YOU, your own Inner Authority, and it will guide you wisely if you listen.

Chapter 11

Are You a Mutant? The Three Major Human Design Circuit Groups

Individuals (Mutants) are agents of chaos... and when living correctly, are energetically guiding others towards higher order.
Davidian Lyon

There are three major Circuit groups in the Human Design chart. Understanding these dynamics is game-changing and eye-opening not only in your own life but also when understanding and operating with others out there in the world.

Just as a caveat, I am breaking this down very simply; there are many more distinctions and subgroups as well as streams involved in this topic. For the sake of letting this information be explained in a way that everyone can utilize it, I am going to break this down in the most basic elucidation.

The Three Major Circuit Groups in the Human Design Rave Chart

To see where these Channels are in your chart, don't forget your accompanying PDF so you can look at your chart and follow along.

1. **Individual, which includes:** Integration/The Centering Circuit/The Knowing Circuit
2. **Tribal, which includes:** The Defense Circuit/The Ego Circuit
3. **Collective, which includes:** The Logic Circuit/The Abstract Circuit

Each of us will have several Gates in all of these areas. You want to add up how many Channels or Gates you have in each location for the fun of this discussion. The place where you have most of your Gates and Channels might just be the type of energy you relate to the most. Like most of my clients, we also see many people who are engaged in different energies that are not correct for them. For instance, it might be a big AHA moment for someone with all Individual Circuitry – Mutant energy, we like to say :) – who has been raised in tribal religious organizations or in a large corporation where their Individuality is not recognized. So understanding this might assist people with some significant insights, particularly on why they may have felt like black sheep in the family, outsiders, or might feel like they are in the wrong place. So let's get into it.

The Individual Circuitry

So, let me share a bit of a story here. Imagine a young nerdy type who did not fit in at school. This young nerd (said in the most endearing tone) was super smart. No one got him, and he could not explain his particular genius to classmates, family members, or even his teachers. So, he locked himself in a garage and began tinkering with some technology that he imagined could change the world one day.

He went into his garage every day after school; his friends and family didn't understand him at all, even made fun of his ideas. He didn't care too much; he was into what he was doing, separated himself from the tribe, and was content doing his crazy thing in the garage even if no one knew what he was doing. (Anyone else thinking of that song, *What's He Building in There...* yeah, me too, works perfectly here. The Tom Waits song; no, not the TikTok meme, LOL.) He was kind of seen as a bit of a freak. Until one day, one friend recognized his genius.

So, he let this friend into the garage and showed him what he was building.

That friend immediately saw the genius of the invention.

This friend decided that he wanted to join in on this garage adventure as well. So, now the two of them went every day after school to the garage to tinker away.

Eventually, these two were ready to bring this invention out to the tribe.

So, first, we have a mutant that doesn't fit in, then we have the first earliest adopter who could SEE the Individual. So, with this, we have the person with Individual Circuitry separating himself from the Tribal Circuitry and one of the tribe members now spotting early genius.

It will still take a while for the rest of the tribe to get it.

But you see, this friend knew where to bring this wild invention that the two of them were now both spending day in and day out tinkering away on. This friend knew to bring the brand new fantastic invention to another early adopter.

So, he brought it out to the first store that sold – you guessed it, the first Apple computer.

Yes, Steve Wozniak was the above Individual freak (Projector with 43-23 the Individual Channel of Structuring we lovingly call, Freak to Genius Channel) and Steve Jobs the first person who recognized him. The idea was to really show the connection, flow, and need for all three of the major Circuitry the need and separation of the Individual, the Tribal, and the sharing to the Collective, not to go deeply into each of their charts.

For this crazy idea to be entirely accepted by the tribe and hit the larger collective, it would have to go through many iterations, tinkering, adjusting and then perfecting the innovation. But eventually, this Individual would mutate the entire tribe with this innovative invention. It would eventually be accepted by the tribe and then spread to the greater collective and shift the world. For the tribe to grow and innovate, it needs the Individual to not fit in, to rebel, and even to threaten the very existence of the tribe by not following tribal laws, to live a unique life, and go their own way.

In a nutshell, this is how the Individual/Tribal/Collective Circuitry operates. So, thank you, Steve Wozniak and Steve Jobs, for this excellent example of Circuitry, oh, and also for revolutionizing the planet with the unbelievable invention you started in your garage.

So, let's recap. All the Circuits are essential; we all have a combination of these energies. Each is needed to make society run. It is super helpful to see these Aura Mechanics operating in our own lives and in our families. If you don't have many Individual Circuits, you are still unique. Not one chart is the same, and there are 100,000s of variations on each chart, like viewing the DNA strands of each person. So technically, to answer the question – Yes, we are all mutants. However, those with many Channels in the Individual arena may more deeply feel afflicted by the characteristics I discuss below.

The Individual: So, the Individual will feel a little like an outsider; they won't understand why they don't fit into a group. They might think, why is it even in my own family, I am seen as an outsider or the black sheep? Why do I feel like a full-time interloper, never a member when I go to any type of event or group of any kind?

Usually, these people also suffer from the theme of melancholy. A melancholy that has an essential purpose in human evolution is not depression if appropriately handled. Counter to popular Manifestation ideas, this melancholy adds to innovation. If the Individual doesn't try and stuff it down or tell themselves that this is a horrible feeling, just give me the antidepressants so I can fit in.

No, stuffing down the melancholy isn't the best approach. The Individual must feel this melancholy, use it as a muse for innovation, and know you are meant to be different! Are you starting to see why just the basics of this intel might change your life?

You might not fit into your family, your religion, your group, your community. You might always feel like an outsider, but you are needed for human evolution so honor your uniqueness! The Individual threatens the tribe. Anyone who comes in with their ideas, beliefs, or way of doing things shakes up the group's rules. It doesn't matter which group you belong to, a family, religion, school system, corporate system; all of these tribal organizations need you to follow their tribal guidelines, or you threaten the very foundation they have been built on. But adhering to the tribal rule is death to the Individual, slow soul-crushing for those with Individual Circuitry. They are not here to follow the laws of the tribe; they are designed to bust them open.

Of course, this is not always comfortable for the Individual, particularly if they don't know their Human Design and are not able to appreciate their uniqueness. It is painful to always feel like an outsider who doesn't fit in. So, most Individuals will medicate, snuff out their unique vibe, bend over backward and do whatever is necessary to be liked, accepted, or included in the tribe. Hence why we are a community of homogenized people. Not being accepted is so very painful and let's just say the tribe is lovely if you are in it, but despicable to you once you break the rules, follow your way of thinking, or live by your unique way of being. For most Individuals, they meet this information thinking something is seriously wrong with them. Asking why they never fit in. Why life is so difficult and complicated for them. Most will cut off aspects of themselves to be liked, valued, or appreciated by the tribe but conversely affect the very thing that makes them different.

Tribal Circuitry

Now, this is where all of the tribe lives. The Tribal Circuitry is the family, government, business, education system, making and raising the babies, love, sex, religion, war, any group organization. These energies are found here in Tribal Circuitry.

Rules of the tribe are set by the tribe. The tribe absolutely loves and nurtures those people in the tribe. They want you to join in! They want you to accept their ideology, their belief systems, their rules, and regulations. They will welcome you in with loving arms as long as you follow their tribal rules.

Yes, they can be seen as the most loving people around, to those in their tribe only. They will care for the wounded, take in the poor, put food in a starving man's belly – for those in the group – until you break their rules. You see, the tribe is also the most vicious group when you go against them. Think about every major religious war, think of the cult behavior if you want out, think of your family when you bring up a heated topic and get banned from the dinner table. Think of the religion that banishes a family member if they are not part of the religion anymore. The Individual threatens the tribe, period.

The tribe's very foundation cannot survive if they accept an Individual who challenges their beliefs. But unfortunately, the Individual is designed to stand up against the tribe. You see, just as dangerous as the Individual is to the tribe, the tribal ways are hazardous to the Individual. They have to live as themselves, in their unique way. Otherwise, they suffer a lifetime. And suffering is what most of these Individuals are taught to do. Just conform, stuff it down. They are told not to be themselves but to cut parts of themselves off to fit into the tribe, until NOW.

We are here to help the Individual free him or herself from the Tribal rule, to know they were never designed to FIT IN. Busting free serves everyone, and even though the tribe fights it, it serves the tribe as well from stagnation and inbreeding. The tribe needs the Individual. So the tribe gains from learning tolerance as well.

I am not Tribe bashing. I have a lot of Tribal energy myself, and I love the Tribe as long as they recognize the parts of myself that are Individual. You see, we all have all of these aspects within us. So, it helps to understand how these energies operate to support each other in being our unique selves.

Also, this information may help the tribe recognize the Individual ideas as necessary for tribal growth and begin the process of allowing people to think for themselves.

You see, as we head towards 2027, this is going to happen whether the Tribe likes it or not. Tribal Aura Mechanics that once held all of the Tribal groups together will not be there anymore. So, it's time we all get used to this shift and prepare for it. Families, companies, religions, governments, banks, and all of the tribal systems will be forced to reinvent themselves. Ask yourself if you are part of a tribe, and because of the group dynamic, have you inadvertently disavowed the Individual? The values of the tribe need to be called into scrutiny, for there is a reordering that is happening. So, question your tribal values, and perhaps we can all begin the journey of honoring every person for the unique way they think, see the world, and experience life. Perhaps we can all be encouraged to thrive in our own lane. Maybe we can learn to honor each person for the unique energy they hold, without trying to tell them what to do or control their behavior and/or shunning them if they do not behave in the ways of the tribe. Perhaps this knowledge alone might assist us in moving through some of the painful red and blue wars that this Country mindlessly engages in.

Understanding this knowledge might just allow space for differing opinions, for allowing people to speak for themselves, even if it challenges your tribal belief systems. Maybe we can learn to allow the unique thoughts to rise from each person and, instead of shunning differences, see the beautiful, unique code each person is expressing? Whether you have a lot of Tribal Circuitry or not, we are all unique individuals. Even if we enjoy and fit into tribes, we all have a unique motivation, perception, and way of operating in this world. When we allow each person to express themselves, even within the context of a group dynamic, this freedom is genuine love. All else is control, manipulation, conditional love and causes each person a lifetime of suffering.

The Collective Circuitry

The Collective holds themes of the do-gooders of the world (when they aren't operating out of the shadow). Those with these Circuits will feel a calling to share the higher intel with the world; those people with Collective Circuitry might be driven to serve the greater good for ALL OF HUMANITY CONCERNED.

Those with Collective Circuitry are driven to share the new inventions with everyone, even those who don't have enough money to buy these new computers. They will make the technology accessible for everyone. They see the value in honoring the whole of humanity. They will be bringing new ideas from the tribe out to less fortunate people, setting up the nonprofits feeding the homeless recognizing we all need to be served regardless of class hierarchies.

The Collective feels this incredible drive to share all they have learned.

They will either be driven to learn and share through Abstract experience or through Logic Circuitry, proving knowledge over time through the fundamental scientific hypothesis we all have grown to know and love. This logical thinking has dominated culture for the last 411 years, as discussed in the Cross of Planning and the upcoming shift in 2027. This logic domination is why most people feel things need to be scientifically proven before believing anything. As I stated above, these Aura Mechanics will no longer hold the collective in place. Hence, many people will become disoriented when no one science proves an agreed-upon reality anymore. Watching this logic dismantle is a little like watching the news dispersion during the Trump years and the Pandemic. No one knew what to believe. There was a distortion of fake news, misunderstandings, conspiracies. Basically, there was no logic used to understand the problem. So, what do we do with this? When the bottom falls out of how we have been thinking, understanding reality, and following systems for the last 411 years, we have one thing to fall back on, and that is our

INDIVIDUAL... you guessed it, Strategy and Inner Authority.

Of course, there will still be logic within the collective experience, so you can still use your noggin to think and figure out problems. Logic will still be used; just imagine its value having about as much impact as an Individual knowing had over the last 411 years – smaller than a pot to piss in. Unless, of course, you have been on the fringe and have honored the revelatory teachings of Channels who have direct knowing without understanding how exactly their knowledge has come to be. The truth – this type of knowledge – would be considered Individual. You can see the majority of the Collective did not really value this type of knowledge. If you are like me, however, you have over time cultivated a deep inner discernment compass for esoteric knowledge that was not proven by science. You may already understand how to decipher which of these teachings are valid and worthy. If you aren't like me and rely solely on science, this might be the time to learn how to check-in inwardly for truth. Otherwise, the media shizz show, government shenanigans, agenda-driven propaganda leadership, paid news, Internet-controlled information will have your head spinning, not knowing which way is up.

Imagine a world where people not only look to their inner knowing for guidance and confirmation, but each one of us respects the knowledge and inner knowing of the other person. MIND BLOWN!

So, this Collective Circuitry has contributed immensely and will continue to be part of the human experience. The Collective sharing and gathering of information for the good of the whole are shown by systems like the Internet, nonprofit organizations, infrastructure of our highways, to name a few. So, all of these things are important; this Collective Circuitry and sharing do serve humanity well.

Those with more Collective Circuitry will also not fit into the tribe or understand how tribal law operates. They will rise above and wish to share for the greater good of humanity and not as driven by the money or the Ego. Why nonprofits were born.

The Collective and the Tribal Circuitry both dominated the Cross of Planning and the operating Aura Mechanics for the world over the last cycle. As we see this dismantling, what are you noticing? As we look back to contemplate these energies over the previous 411 years, does this make sense to you? Can you see how the Logic, the Collective, and the Tribe towered over the Individual? Especially important to witness it and notice if you see this happening in the world around you. It helps to have systems of understanding as things change, dismantle, and potentially break down into unknown directions. When we systematically know what is going on and have a way to understand this shift, we can harmoniously navigate these changing times and rocky waters with insight, compassion, and clarity.

Chapter 12

The Law of Attraction & Why Manifestation Does Not Work for Every Type

True elegance for me is the manifestation of an independent mind.
Isabella Rossellini

In this chapter, we will be discussing manifestation from the Human Design perspective and why the Law of Attraction and manifestation don't work for every Type.

So, this might shock a few of you die-hard Manifestation Boss Babe Junkies, like me. I consider myself to come from this arena, and I have studied this energy intensely and used it to manifest many things in my life. Unfortunately, at the height of my career, I realized having everything I wanted was super unfulfilling, and I was unhappy, so very darkly depressed.

Having what you THINK YOU WANT does not always bring the fulfillment you think you will get when you have it. So, this is the first thing you must note as we dive into this topic.

Next, we all have different Signature themes to strive for depending on your Type. When you allow yourself to surrender to this, there is a profound unfolding that begins to happen. Do things manifest for all Types, absolutely! However, it just might be in a way you can't plan, it might be in a direction you would never have guessed, and it just might take a lot less energy than you imagined. Can I get an Amen or happy dance GIF?

So, if I were to tell you for the Projectors you would have Success, Generators and MGs you would have Satisfaction, Manifestors Peace and Reflectors Awe, would that work for you? Sometimes our Manifestors are making so much shizz happen, but they don't even realize that making something happen is not the end game for them; it is Peace. That is a game-changer.

So, first, you must feel if you are hitting on your Signature theme; if not, your manifestations might not just be wrought with outward "success" but inner pain?

Lastly, and this is super crucial regarding manifestation, not all manifestation tips will work for everyone (every Type) across the board. It is about understanding what is correct for you, why things will work for others, and sorting through the tips and tools based on what is in alignment with your uniqueness.

So let's take this one step deeper and compare some standard techniques from Manifestation or Law of Attraction and let me break it down for you as to WHY it will not work for every Type:

The Myth-Busting of the Manifestation Game

Before I get into it, I want you to know I am a big proponent of Manifestation tools, but only when you know your unique Design first!

Feeling aligned: This is one of the most significant components of the LOA; when you feel aligned with wealth, it will begin to appear. It is not about seeing is believing: it is about believing and feeling first, then you will bring this desire to fruition. The Manifestation arena breaks this down into feeling groovy first, and then your desires will follow.

If you have negative feelings or pain, stress, anxiety, your first step is to feel better.

Well, here is the Human Design problem with this.

Melancholy is a part of many people's Design, and it is needed as a catalyst for not only spiritual development but also creative inspiration. Also, if you are Emotional, you must feel your feelings entirely. If you try too hard to shift out of the lower waves without touching them entirely, you will actually cut off those lower tone waves so needed for introspection and inspiration. So, melancholy is part of the Individual Circuitry. Everyone will have at least one Gate in this Individual Circuit, and some people will have many or all of their Channels in the Individual Circuitry. So, suppose you are told not to feel melancholy or deep feelings because it will take you off the frequency of alignment. In that case, you run the risk of vast aspects of your uniqueness being untapped. The depths of stirring mutation energy are then repressed and might perhaps translate into negative self-harming outlets.

With this said, it is crucial to not put the feeling barometer on the chart of high/low or good/bad. Our best suggestion is to feel everything fully! Don't just shoot to be in the highest alignment all the time, don't be afraid of the melancholy moments if you are Individual or you are Emotional. You must feel all of your feelings entirely and not make a story up about why you are feeling high or low, but allow it to catapult your inspiration and creativity. Do not judge yourself if you feel low. Do not tell yourself why you might feel sad; just allow it all. This is important for these unique, Emotional, and mutant beings. Do not try and force yourself to feel good when you are in a low wave. Trust, allow, feel. If you are down or melancholy, read, write, be creative, let the emotions drive you to create. This will open the cascade of beauty. Trying to stuff down a tsunami does not work, and it might just cause a natural disaster. So, let this energy flow; controlling it will do more harm than good.

Visualize what you want: In the Law of Attraction or other Manifestation tools, they tell you to visualize what it is you want to manifest. Some will tell you to create a vision board, make a list, focus on what you want, not the reality of what you have. In the next chapter, I will go deeper into these specific tools.

But, according to Human Design, your mind does not understand what is best for the life or the vehicle. So, this notion of simply visualizing what you want would lead you astray from what is meant to manifest in your life. The idea of Human Design manifestation comes from trusting your Strategy and unique Inner Authority to lead you to the correct life for you, a life you will love! My suggestion is to notice where you might be visualizing something specific that is against your Inner Authority. Some of you are here to be more Specific Manifestors, and some are meant to be more Passive Manifestors, and I will go into this in the next chapter. Also, a big issue with visualizing something you want is that your mind might be sabotaging these possibilities because of past trauma, pain, or negative habitual patterns of thought due to your conditioning. These spirals can keep you in a loop.

Let me give you a tangible example: if you are losing money, or a deal/investment went south, or you have past money trauma (yup, you guessed it, I'm speaking from experience), and you ruminate over the loss, you become a victim. You might play out negative scenarios over and over again in your mind. This absolutely might keep you out of the flow of life and manifestation, even with the best visualizations or vision boards. The idea here is to pay attention to where the Not-Self mind is counteracting any visualizations. In other words, there is an endless sea of different million-dollar ideas that may come into inspiration for you, but if your mind conditioning does not believe you are worthy, all visioning is out the window. As you experiment with these new ideas of Responding and waiting for the Invitation, then LIFE will bring what is correct for you, and any visions your mind thought were perfect for you just might be expanded into better options. Where strictly Human Design information can keep you stuck is not realizing that you do hold power in your focus and attention. If your mind is habitually in trauma or a past pattern, you need to shift this focus into a more positive groove by actively being aware of this spiral. I am also a big proponent of healing work to lift out of any trauma. Placing the attention on higher-minded positive energy like an infinite possibility and universal intelligence, you shift the energy then more positive things will be brought into your Auric field. So, there is a dance with the Inner Authority. The main distinction is if the mind controls what you want and visualizes the exact outcome, you might miss the opportunity and power to allow the higher divine forces or infinite intelligence to lead the way! Also, we must note that the mind is a great hindrance to all manifestations, and keeps you in a pattern of deep conditioning. So in Human Design, our goal is to let the MIND become a back seat passenger who can watch the world as the vehicle intelligence of the Inner Authority takes the wheel. This magical shift opens doors you might have never imagined and creates a super-fun ride along the way.

Meditation: It is stated in most spiritual communities that meditation is a tool that will work for everyone the same way for healing, calming the mind, stepping into a higher frequency, awakening higher potential, and stepping into new dimensions of energy.

I love meditation. I believe it has served me immensely. I am designed (this is due to my Undefined Head and Ajna and Meditation Tone in my View) to thrive with meditation tools.

However, when it comes to meditation, some people are going to have an easier time with this than others. Those people with a Defined Head might have trouble silencing or clearing the mind, and they might need to do other forms of meditation like art, walking, or just getting so in the zone that their mind relaxes. Or they might need a specific type of energetic upliftment in their meditations that only they relate to. In other words, not all meditations are created alike. If those with a Defined Head or Ajna can learn to hone in and focus on the proper energetic alignment, they often become very clear meditators or channelers but it usually takes finding the right meditation.

There is also a Tone "Meditation," an advanced part of the Human Design chart where we explore the Human Design

Diet/the Environment/the View/the Motivation based on your Human Design chart. Those people with Meditation as part of their unique View are designed to use meditation to help them perceive correctly. These areas are another layer deeper beneath the surface that exposes our uniqueness. We are not all designed to view the world the same way, eat the same, live in the same environment, or meditate the same way. The tiny suburban houses condition us, but this notion of all humans living in the same type of dwelling is not correct for most people. So, also our meditation tools and techniques will vary by Design.

We are all unique and designed to live in our unique way. I know, shocking! Imagine a world where we all had individual dwellings, ate in our way not dictated by the food pyramid with agendas of selling more bread to the masses This has to do with your Design Diet and Environment, which are not topics I will cover this this book (check the PDF for more on Diet/Environment). The point is, there is no one way to live, or to meditate. So, I encourage you to discover how to quiet the mind, meditate, connect with higher vibrational frequency based on your unique way of unifying with the divine source.

Imagine a world where we were free to be ourselves – how unbelievably magical would that be. Well, that is the incredible gift this material is serving up to humanity. So, with all of this said, even though meditation appears to serve all of humanity on the path of enlightenment, some people are more appropriately designed to benefit from meditation than others.

The point here, some people are designed to thrive in meditation, and some will struggle. So once again, we debunk that meditation works the same for everyone. This guidance will serve those with a Defined Head or Ajna not to just shut down meditation, but understand that a little more searching for the proper alignment will help their Type. There is more to be said on this; for example, those Defined Head and Ajna might also be better at channeling direct energies without the confusion an Open Head will experience. (As a fun fact, Esther Hicks has a Defined Head and Ajna, and I often see this in those who can directly channel without distraction.) There are nuances of connecting to a higher source, meditation, and understanding these frequencies based on how our Design operates. So, knowing your uniqueness first will really serve all of the Law of Attraction tools you are coming across.

Receive information from a download and take action: This is a super common practice amongst most of the spiritual communities I have been involved with. I have done this myself many times, and it has gotten me into immensely troubling situations in my life. In many spiritual communities people will have an energetic opening, connection to a guide, angel, higher self, and have a potent download of information or guidance on the direction to take next. Most people see this type of information to hold an incredible amount of value and guidance for their life. I am not debunking the power of downloads. I have them many times, along with channeling and other connections to the Galactic Federations and beings of light. The key difference here that Human Design can assist us in understanding is that these downloads are not meant for immediate action.

After paying close attention to the chapters above, we know that only 8% of the population is designed to initiate or take action. So, any Generators, Manifesting Generators, Projectors or Reflectors who get powerful downloads, no matter what source this is coming from, acting on it will not work. No matter which guide, which angel, which enlightened insight – any one of these Types who gets an idea and goes out immediately to make it happen will suffer. So, this is often the place of the most confusion from the spiritual community.

We are all taught to meditate, look inside, catch the inspirational vision, or download material and then go out and create this.

In Human Design, we are aware that we all have pressure from the Head and the Root to go out and make shizz happen, but the BIG TRICK here is to not act out on this pressure. To be able to learn to find the miracle in the waiting. This takes a lot of courage to wait and to live your Design.

However, suppose you can utilize some of these ideas, like vibrating at a higher frequency, aligning to the energy of wealth, and learning how to utilize your unique strategy and Inner Authority? In that case, you can powerfully integrate these Law of Attraction tools for your Aura Type. Success is so much easier when you are willing to combine all these mystical tools into your life.

Many other self-help LOA tips will not work for most of the population. Here are some of the most popular:

- Follow your heart.
- Do what you love, and the money will follow.
- Any type of motivational tip around, go out and make it happen, just do it; you have what it takes. Anything that encourages you to push beyond your limitations. I know these are all well-meaning inspirations, but these are also OUTDATED concepts.
- Spontaneous decisions are essential to make.
- Get out there and hustle to your goals.
- Any cookie-cutter system for funnels, e-mails, FB ads, etc., may work for some but not all.
- Just listen to your intuition.
- Wake up early, work out, get motivated first thing in the morning.

Some people are designed to move slowly, even to be "lazy," so if you are watching these types of motivational tips, you quite literally might feel horrible about yourself if you cannot keep up.

So, I am officially letting you off the hook. Your only

objective now, if you want to live as your authentic self, is to follow your unique Inner Authority. Let go of all other self-help motivational tools that are incorrect for you. Those can throw you off from YOUR OWN TRIP. Most people have created some type of push, and they may succeed with it to varying degrees. They then push it onto other people and force others to move forward in a direction that is not correct for them. With all of that said of course, if you find yourself not reaching any goals, watching too much TV, involved with any type of addiction, unable to take action of any kind, you might be facing other types of issues. So do not just use your Human Design as an excuse to engage in abusive, self-indulgent, or self-medicating behavior. We still need to all be aligned to health, inspiration, well-being, self-care, and then living correctly as yourself will be the exact piece to assist you.

If you are one to make excuses often to keep yourself small, limited, or in victim consciousness, and you are using your Human Design as an excuse, please take note. There is a difference. Having an awareness that a dolphin is not designed to fly and yet complaining all day you can't fly and forcing yourself to try and taking flying lessons just won't help. Know yourself, get in the water if you are a dolphin, follow the guidance, and don't try to be something you are not.

So, as you can see, most of the motivational, self-help gurus might just create a world of confusion. Notice if any teachers are encouraging you to be something you are not. If they are forcing you to do things that don't feel aligned for you, and then possibly making you feel shame, bad, or less than for not living up to their expectations, this is a prescription for suffering.

Do not let anyone push their trip onto you. The greatest gift you can give yourself is self-love, believing in your uniqueness, understanding and studying your chart, and following your own GPS system.

How to Use Human Design in Accordance with LOA to Manifest by Design and the Spiritual Awakening We Are Witnessing

If you understand it from a full spectrum of each person's uniqueness, I believe that the Law of Attraction (you can also include any self-help, motivational, or spiritual tools) has an essential impact on us. Of course, for those who know this Law, it is ALWAYS working. However, if you do not understand the Human Design dynamic, you just might be inadvertently pushing your dreams out of reach without understanding exactly which part of the methods are not working. Then, of course, we just have a lot of bitter Projectors and Frustrated Generators, super angry Manifestors, and disappointed Reflectors who do not believe any of this woo-woo crap. If we explore it with your Strategy in mind, you just might open doors you thought were forever off limits to you!

So let's start from the beginning. I believe that we are vibrational beings. We live in a vibrational universe, and we are also extensions of source energy. Some people say this as, "We are spiritual beings having a human experience." This is aligned with science, quantum physics, and any modern-day understanding of how the Universe operates. But what does this mean in practice?

As you wait and experiment with your Aura Mechanics, you will then need to understand the frequency and vibrational levels of your thoughts. The spiritual element is essential and not mentioned in the Human Design community because Ra Uru Hu, the founder, really did not want any practitioners to speak about the spiritual or mystical element of Human Design. He wanted people to try on the strategy and decide for themselves if it had value. I love this notion Ra had, and it was important when he brought the information forward. It helped people get out of spiritual, mystical trappings we have seen many a guru fall into. The spiritualized ego, the my way is better than your way. The spiritual traps are so vast, deep, and complicated, of course, it is too much to dig into here. But with this system, it is personality-less, meaning it is not based on a specific guru or teacher. (Let's hope the Human Design tribe doesn't also fall too deep into the cult-like Tribal way of controlling all the intel since Ra has died – there is irony in trying to control information that tells you to honor and follow your INNER AUTHORITY ONLY.) Anyway, I digressed again for a moment. Because the spiritual element is not often mentioned in Human Design, it is my job to incorporate it here, embody it into these teachings, and share them both, assuming we all want to live our most fulfilled life. This intel is simple, straightforward, and it takes it out of the personalized drama and leads us into a neutral space of the passenger. This passenger consciousness is not personal; it aligns to a higher vibrational intelligence called vehicle intelligence. We all get there in very different and unique ways; this is a piece of the puzzle we need to incorporate into the spiritual teachings.

Even when you look at the dismantling of tribes, it is not personal. It is not necessarily an evil Cabal creating the breakdown. (I am not saying it doesn't exist personally; I live in the "I don't Know" on that one.) But what I am saying is the Aura Mechanics are not personal; it is just the wheel moving and life-changing. Now, we also need to understand that there are spiritual teachings that are actually important. Spiritual awakened masters are NOT a religion. I see Human Design teachers lump spiritual teaching and mysticism with religious dogma. Awakened masters are not in the same category as organized religions. Awakened masters, in my humble opinion, are also not those who have had a drug-induced experience that tapped them into wisdom beyond this dimension. These teachers have been able to rise above the third-dimensional limited perceptions of the world through lifetimes of cultivating inner awareness and transformation of the limited perception of the mind. These fantastic beings can create realities in the higher frequency expression and are real, and many are leading this world silently with elegance. My point, high level spiritual teachings will not be overlooked in my integration of Human Design. If people seriously want to live their highest life expression (I am assuming most of you are with me on the importance of this as a life mission), they must be merged. So how do we do this?

Exploring the Vibrational Influence on Your Design:

- Spiritual influence is the unseen forces through us and around us that connect to our vibrational nature.

- Your thoughts align you to experiences. In other words, whatever habitual patterns of beliefs you have running through your mind will bring you a reflection of those thoughts in your reality. So, it is imperative to create a higher vibe thought to assist you in living out a heavenly existence on this planet, or else your thoughts on autopilot lead you to a painful reality.

- The reason for existence is not to win with stuff or outer achievements: it is to awaken mastery of living in a human body while connected fully to your higher-self which is rooted in love, compassion, wholeness, forgiveness, and a profound connection with the source of nameless and control-less God.

- When your mind runs amok with no awareness of what it is doing, it will have fragments of conversations, ruminate over past events, stress over what has to happen next. Your mind, without awareness, will think about what you did wrong that day, all of your mistakes, it will contemplate past relationships – basically, it is a wild shizzelshow. Most of the time it leads to breakdown, panic, anxiety, depression, psychological pain, and dysfunction.

- From the Human Design perspective, this is the Undefined Centers talking to you with all the conditioning of the planet from parents, friends, teachers, etc.

- Passenger consciousness is a beautiful tool to implement; it guides you to a life you were born for.

- However, if the mind continues to chatter, which it will inevitably do, you can also transform the mind's chatter to align with higher frequency and vibrational commentary, as well as pure silence.

- These keynotes, my friend, can change your life. This is a piece the Human Design puzzle misses and an essential missing link for those just studying Human Design.

This vibrational awareness of thought and alignment is critical to integrate into this intel. A lot of people do not realize we have a choice about the direction of our inner voice. Or often, in Human Design, this is confused with the notion that when you discover your unique Aura Mechanics, you have no choice but to surrender the mind and follow your Inner Authority. All I can say about this dichotomy is that both things are true. The mind is complex. If you can silence the mind and ride as a passenger, bravo, you are probably among a select few, shining a beacon of hope to humanity. You might be few and far between. So, I find it essential to mention that most of us need to understand the difference between allowing the negative mind to proliferate or inserting this loop with a freshwater splash of new thought. As we align to our Design, we begin this journey of awakening. However, the mind is a mighty monkey, so it is vital to understand the more profound ways it sabotages your growth. By understanding that we first need to become aware of the mind, then allow it to take the back seat while simultaneously inserting more high-vibe aligned thoughts, we can powerfully awaken to our highest potential as humans in this time. So, you got it? If so, you are probably awakening to enlightenment status right now as we speak.;) Or you're like, if this girl knew what crazy nonstop manic thoughts are going on full-time in my mind, she would be stunned and shocked into hysteria and awe at the same time. I speak from experience.

From the spiritual perspective, there are tools to assist you in reprograming the mind. Awareness is the first step. Vehicle intelligence or Aura Mechanics (Human Design) is an experiential mental realm. So combining these two arenas is magical!

- Please note: If you have a trauma or a wound from the past, this takes a more profound healing journey. I recommend if you need healing to go to a spiritual psychology therapist. If you have any type of experience that may have caused emotional or mental trauma, pain, or PTSD, there are many tools for healing. You can live a beautiful free life with the right tools. The only way to heal the mind is through spiritual awakening tools that can transcend the mind. If you choose to continue to try and heal the mind through any intellectual work, you will just be adding a maze into a maze. Check the PDF for more tools and references.

If we learn anything from Human Design, we learn extreme patience as we wait to Respond or wait for the Invitation or the entire 28-day cycle. As we wait, we must align our frequency and thoughts, drawing in the invitations or circumstances to respond to. This higher divine alignment takes practice and keen insight into who we are and what we think about.

There is one more point that I feel is important to discuss when contemplating Human Design and spirituality. This concept of no-choice. From my understanding of working and studying in the world of metaphysics, I witnessed many explanations of the times we are in. Looking at these changing times from the Human Design perspective, we see the Aura Mechanics shifting of the wheel, which explains so much. We can also look at this from a more extensive shift cycle, moving from a 3rd-density world to a 4th-density world (NOT to be confused with the fourth dimension). Densities are a little different than our understanding of dimensions. This principle explained in *The Law of One,* a "PhD" level download on spiritual potentialities, is a text I often reference for more profound spiritual wisdom of the world. One of the most important notions in this *Law of One* text is that this changing of the wheel includes a choice by humanity to graduate to fourth density or 5th-dimensional life here on earth.

Most people are unaware of this choice and will continue to live in a 3rd-dimensional world. If you understand we are shifting, and you are aware of the co-creative power of your life, then the choice becomes very real. It is the choice of whether you will be in the camp of service to self or choose the service to others. *The Law of One* is a long and complex spiritual teaching. We'll break this down, so you can contemplate this choice now. Simply put – are you going to satisfy all of your human desires with greed, control, manipulation to manifest your own ends, and be a dick about it? Or are you going to align into realizing the true joy is knowing we are all one, and as you serve the other, you serve the whole? There is no sacrificing of your Inner Authority here, which is why I love Human Design. This notion works so well with knowing your Inner Authority. When we think of service to others, we often think of being a doormat and just giving over our will to another. But alas, it is not this at all. It is about being true to who you are and 100% allowing others to be true to themselves while learning kindness, compassion, and naturally aligning to serve. Because when you are connecting to the true love source, this connection is entirely and 100% satisfying. It fills every need and joy, and heals every wound mentally and physically as you are drinking full-time from the sparkling clean well of the source. When you have it all, the heart's desire is only to serve.

Those who stay ambivalent about the need for clarification in their human experience and do not choose will continue in the 3rd density. The idea is like either you graduate to college, or you stay in high school. I do feel it is important to note here as we discuss spiritual principles. The choice/no choice can get confusing for people. So, according to Ra Uru Hu, the notion of NO CHOICE is about your Design being unchanging and ever-present throughout a life. You are who you are, you have a life path, and as we surrender to it, we align to that path. For many Human Design practitioners, this bleeds into the notion that you have no choice in how to *BE* on your journey. In *The Law of One*, this choice is either serving the self's needs, desires and wants, or serving others. Those of you looking for guidance on stepping into alignment of serving others, dedicating for the good of the whole above and beyond selfish needs, you are my peeps. This means you know the truth that we are all one consciousness beyond the flesh; when we help another, we help ourselves. If you are someone interested in serving the self path, this is not your book and will not help you. Helping another is not based on only serving those with the same values, religion, color, status. It is not about only helping those from whom you can get something back. It is an unconditional love for humanity. When we are humble servants, the world heals, and we can awaken to greater heights within humanity. Of course, we need to understand the boundaries and follow our sovereign Inner Authority first. We also need to understand that to serve the other is to do so by 100% allowing others to embody their own free will. To empower each person to take back their power from anything they have given it to, and teach them that they are the sovereign force of their own lives and their own decision making. This is what Human Design is here to do! These two principles do support each other in spiritual development and are essential to contemplate on this path of becoming our true selves.

All choices are honored and respected without judgment.

So, next, I am going to help you specify the types of ways each of us might benefit even more deeply from integrating the Law of Attraction tools. So, if you feel ready, pull out your charts once again, and I will see you in the next chapter.

Chapter 13

Specific and Non-Specific Manifestors

We must let go of the life we planned, so as to accept the one waiting for us. I don't have faith I have experience.
Joseph Campbell

Specific vs. Non-Specific Manifestors is a term that many Human Design practitioners picked up somewhere along the way to explain different manifestation styles based on your Design. The big question, according to Human Design now: Is this even a thing? This concept did not come from Ra Uru Hu himself, but many people mention this, so I thought it might be good to point it out here while discussing manifestations. Many people are so pressured to manifest, and yet, have no idea how to do this. They watch *The Secret*, listen to YouTube videos, try out techniques and fail, and usually simply give up. This does not have to be the case, and I am going to help crack this code for you, even more deeply in this chapter. So, Ra Uru Hu talks about manifesting taking place in the Throat Center, which I will go into shortly. So who started this Specific Non-Specific, and will it help you manifest? Once again, the more we understand how our Aura Mechanics operate, the more quickly we can sort through all the messages around manifestation, self-help, coaching, and all the confusing ideas we receive out there in the world. Oh, and I don't know who started this. But let's have some fun discussing this controversial aspect of Human Design!

Part of the reason this is controversial is that many Human Design guides feel when you have "no-choice" and are letting the vehicle ride on the monopole through life then, what is there to manifest? So, manifesting by Design simply means so that we can be on the same page for the sake of this discussion, either awakening within your given Rave Chart the highest articulation or living the shadow expression of your chart. You have an influence within the permanence of who you are.

When all of these Human Design concepts in my book (literally and figuratively) are adequately integrated, then these Law of Attraction and the Specific Non-Specific tools will work. Not everyone sees it in this way. Once again, try it on, if it works use it. No need to intellectually debate this stuff. Let's face it, we all want a life that works for us.

In your chart in the Personality Nodes, you will notice an arrow that will either be pointing to the left or the right. You might need the Advanced chart to find these arrows (check PDF for guide). These arrows referred to as Variable in Human Design located in the Personality Nodes are referred to as The View or Perspective. So this concept of Variable is quite an Advanced notion in Human Design. It often does not come into play until you genuinely understand how to live your Strategy and Inner Authority. After you have been living this experiment, it guides you to the right environment. You will then digest life correctly, and then, and only then, will you see the world accurately. Once you View the world correctly, then we enter the notion of Variable.

We see the notion of Specific and Non-Specific comes here in the Variable of View. I am mentioning this even though it is complicated because I want to share this concept before diving in. The idea of Specific Non-Specific is a watered-down simplified perspective of View – but I think it has a powerful impact. Some super die-hard Human Design guides just might disagree with me here, but we are all allowed to THINK FOR OURSELVES. So, I just recommend that you experiment with this to see if this is true for you.

If your arrow is to the left, you are a Specific Manifestor, and if you have an arrow pointing to the right, you are a Non-Specific Manifestor. Please note this is just referring to your manifestation style, not your Human Design Aura Type.

Please note this DOES NOT change the fact that only 8% of the population are "Manifestors." This is saying that we are all designed for practicing the Law of Attraction or manifestation differently. We are all different, so don't get bogged down by the titles.

On the advanced chart, you are looking at the Personality Nodes Arrow, the North and South Nodes on the Personality or the Black side of the chart.

When there is a right-pointing arrow, this is known as being Passive and it is future oriented. This means people with this right-pointing arrow have more of an ability to understand the future and forward-thinking trends. The left is known as Active, you are more comfortable with the traditional way of manifesting and focused on the past. You might do better by being more specific and strategic and adhering to the old way of doing things. This is not wrong. Neither are BETTER. It just helps to understand and witness these tendencies within you.

The left-pointing arrow or the Specific Manifestor is going to do better in being more strategic about what they are visioning and wanting to bring into their life. This is specific and is more about the old traditional ways of making something happen out there in the world. You know, get a clear focus, actively move forward, vision the outcome, be guaranteed on its success, believe it, achieve it.

Specific Manifestors-Active

These types of tools will work well for the Left-pointing arrow in Personality North and South Node:

- Making lists, being strategic, planning, focusing, reaching out to the goal
- Lasering more on specific outcomes
- Setting direct and clear goals

- Concentrating on the exact manifestation
- Getting explicit, precise, scrupulous on vision
- Making vision boards
- Having a plan laid out
- Having step by steps to reach a particular goal
- Write out what you want to manifest, be active with each step, have a specific plan, create a chart, know the strategic steps
- Being a little more masculine (in how we traditionally viewed the masculine way of going out and concurring)

This direct, focused, forceful action to make dreams a reality is how we have historically been operating as a society. This dominated action has caused some beautiful things in the world, and unfortunately, it has also caused a lot of harm. Brute force does make things happen but at what cost? Does the mind/ego drive know what the sacred purpose of your life has in store for you? Humanity is moving more towards power through flow and connection, where no harm is caused, where the greatest good for all of humanity is considered when the individual is setting a goal. This right-facing flow is now coming in to introduce a new way to manifest in the sea of "Let's just take what we want and make shit happen." So, maybe this focused drive isn't what is needed for society's future?

Humanity is moving towards the Right-facing arrow, and eventually, we will all be facing right in the future. We, all of humanity, started Left, meaning we as a people were designed to strategically manifest life. As of right now, we have a combination of both Left and Right arrows, and ultimately, we will all have four Right-facing arrows. Interesting stuff. So, we are currently in this transition in the way we manifest things.

Wow, this transition is causing a mighty stir! Because we have been manifesting through focused action for so long, this shift is not an easy one. Most people are conditioned to believe forcing a dream to happen is the only way to create something. Those who are Right may feel challenged by this at first, not understanding why those old tools of visioning, taking action, making plans will not work for them. So, again, knowing these distinctions serve all of us. We will all eventually need to be open to the flow, the pulse of life force energy that has no specific plan for us. This opening to allowing life's magic without knowing what is next might be terrifying for the Left-past view. So, it is for those people with this new Right energy to bring forward the grace of this change and assist humanity's evolution forward.

The Non-Specific Manifestor-Passive Right-Facing Arrow in the Personality North and South Node

- Focus on the energy, the flow, the feeling rather than the specific outcome.
- Asking for what you want but also claiming all manifestations for the greatest good of all concerned (not just your own ego desire).
- Asking for things that are correct for your Design, beyond what the mind wants.
- Intending for the highest solution for all of humanity in your manifestations.
- Ask yourself, "What does my SOUL actually want?"
- Contemplating, what are you designed for?
- Feel into the energy of your dreams and ALLOW it to unfold.
- Passive is about taking all the energy in, feeling the abundance, magic, success, vision first, then allowing the manifestation to unfold in your life.
- Absorbing peripherally, it might feel vague but allow the feeling of your dream vision in. Revel in the sensation

and let the mystery evolve into magic in your life.

- Sorry, but you might want to throw away all those vision boards, maps, flow charts, specific to do steps towards your dreams, and just let the mystical flow!

If you are Non-Specific, you're here to be more open, receptive, surrendering to the flow rather than focused on a strategic plan. When contemplating your vision or dream, ask from a higher perspective what your soul is longing for, digging in beyond the mind's desires. Your mind thinks it has a grip on what is suitable for your life, but most of the time, it just thinks it knows what is correct for you. This feeling of wanting and knowing exactly what your goals should be is actually part of the conditioning of the planet, so it takes awareness to allow yourself to unplug from this force and open up to the all-knowing field of energetic abundance. Experiment with doing this before your Strategy, meaning this is in the waiting stages. This is the period of creatively brainstorming, working on a website, making the videos, creating content, writing the song, or planning the event, before you Respond or Wait for the Invitation for action. The suggestion for each of you with Right Arrows is to open, allow, think-less, move into the mystery, leap into the field out of your comfort zone, feel into the energy first. Ask spirit what is wanting to birth through your life right now, rather than thinking you know what is next. What are you drawn to, what gifts or questions do people want from you?

The deeper contemplation here on Specific and Non-Specific has more to do with moving away from Past ways of operating and into the future practices of receiving. The Specific manifesting might be more the force, and the surrender of Non-Specific might be experienced as a more feminine life flow. So each of you can now experiment and try to integrate these ideas into your manifestation toolbox. It is a beautiful guide for your individual life; however, it is also a greater contemplation as well for all of humanity and our movement forward. The ultimate consideration here is which has more power, the force of the mind and ego, or the flow of power within the universal frequency. Well, we know which way the Universe and our collective Design is leading humanity.

Chapter 14

Deconditioning – A Power Journey through All Nine Centers

In a toxic family dynamic, the "black sheep" is the one who can see through all the family bullshit.
Author Unknown

You see, all it takes is the readiness to take that journey, to disconnect from the madness of the Not-Self world and its Not-Self purposes to rediscover the dignity of what it is to be you. It is a wonderful thing to love yourself. It truly is magic.
Ra Uru Hu

One of the most critical parts of this system is what we call Deconditioning.

So, let me explain. We are all brought up to believe what we are told. We follow our parents' guidelines, the systems set up by the schools, we listen to TV, our friends, the neighborhood, and we are like sponges absorbing this information. The conditioning element, which is everything around you, forces you in a particular direction regardless of whether it is correct for you or not. So, imagine an assembly line, if you will, you are cogs in a machine, and you are moving forward in that line with a considerable force. Now that you understand a little about how the Penta operates, you then begin to realize that these forces are homogenizing energies, moving us to be alike.

Your family is a Penta, so you are conditioned and homogenized by that energy the minute you are born. Usually, people come to me when they get this gnawing itch that this assembly line is causing pain in the body, stress, boredom, burnout, discomfort, maybe severe illness, or many other symptoms. They know they were designed for something else, but what and how to honor that?

After years of dedicated learnings in various studies, some people who had tried just about everything were at the end of their rope but were still burned out and confused. Many of these dedicated beings tried and read every self-help book, meditated, did yoga, clearings, therapy, NLP, Chakra balancing, tarot readings, energy work, channeling, and nothing seemed to assist them in living a life that worked for them. This is because they were conditioned to believe they were something they were not.

They were healing and clearing the energy that they believed was them, but actually, it was not. They were healing, doing therapy, clearing energy they had absorbed from the other; this energy amplified and distorted by acting like them within their psyche. This is a massive awareness.

This most definitely was the case for me. After years of studying every modality I could get my hands on. After an entire decade of therapy, a Master's in Spiritual Psychology, I still couldn't find a correct career. I still had all my ideas stolen, I was still burned out, I was not seen or understood, but nothing answered these deeper issues.

Why had I been brought down to my knees in confusion after trying, processing and learning so much about myself? Well, I was conditioned to believe that I was a Manifesting Generator, and basically, I was clearing and healing emotional stuff that was not mine over and over again.

It is not something I could have discovered with any other system but this one. Please understand that my Spiritual Psychology Degree was probably one of the most profound periods of my life, and I believe this experience healed me of so much past trauma. Many people in Human Design who have never looked deeply into their past wounds might also be missing some much-needed healing. I know my Master's

Degree in Spiritual Psychology has given me the foundation to understand these teachings fully and to be able to utilize the Human Design teachings on a much more profound level. My point, if you are learning Human Design and you still have trauma responses, broken relationships, and are not able to heal the mind, some deeper psychology, counseling, or spiritual therapy might be needed to get to any extreme past abuse.

But, with Human Design, many issues were solved for me, and I am forever grateful to help people Decondition. It f-ing works, and it is simple, no not easy, but simple.

The Deconditioning process begins in the Centers.

The Centers are sort of a Human Design version of the Chakra system. According to the mythology of this system, we moved from a seven-Centered being (the seven Chakra system) to a nine-Centered being in the late 1700s. This shift moved us out of the mind as the ruling force for human evolution into the vehicle intelligence as the primary source for guidance. This shift is only now starting to be understood, and this nine-Centered being is in desperate need of learning how to operate this human vehicle without the mind.

We have seen concepts like this in many spiritual teachings, including non-duality, when guided or pointed to becoming the witness consciousness.

So, the concept is, this 9-Centered being, which we all are now, has a vehicle intelligence which should be the one controlling the life, making the decisions, and the mind should become the Passenger witnessing life go by. As I mentioned, we see this concept in other spiritual teachings, but we now have the specifics for each person on how to do it.

Why do you want to do it, you ask? Believing that the mind is so intellectual, smart, and has guided us so well as humans, is true. However, now as we evolve, we also realize that the mind, when it runs amok, is a very violent and destructive force. It is corrupting the nature of human evolution. It is time to evolve into a new way of being. This is a robust process of insight and personal discovery. You awaken to WHO YOU REALLY ARE when you allow the mind to do what it is good at, including reading, studying, learning, sharing ideas with others, but not speaking to yourself nonstop all day or making your life decisions. Many people don't enjoy this idea because it's shocking as we reveal all the places inside yourself where you are acting out of the conditioning of the mind. So yes, it is for the brave of heart.

The most important concept I will break down in the following sections is how to understand these Centers based on your specific chart, the right questions to ask yourself to De-condition.

So, if you pull out your chart, you will notice the Centers look like the Chakra system with a couple more Centers added. Again refer to the PDF for images.

You are looking for whether the Center is colored in or white. The color doesn't matter; only if it is white or not. Once you find out which of your Centers are white, you are ready to begin this journey with me below. It is the journey back to yourself, the power journey of Deconditioning.

The basic idea here is that when a Center is white, it is called Undefined or Open (if no hanging Gates at all); this is where you are absorbing, distorting, and amplifying the outside world. In the Centers where you are white, you are susceptible to the conditioning of the planet. These white Centers are your areas of vulnerability.

Now when I say absorb and amplify, contemplate what this might mean for a moment. The energy of the world comes in through that openness referred to as an Undefined Center, with particular attention to that area if it is entirely Open (no hanging Gates), and you take it on believing it is you. It takes an incredibly heightened animated energy in your world, and it feels real. It feels like you – but it is not. You amplify this energy, you misunderstand it, then misinterpret it, and then act out of this distortion.

Please, I beg of you, don't take my word for it. Just contemplate these questions below, and let's see if you relate to any of the Unhealthy aspects of these Centers. Meaning you are living as this blown-up doll-sized expression of yourself, and it is ruling and living your life as you, when it is not. It's kind of like a helium balloon of yourself that takes shape, lifts off, and lives life as you, when it isn't YOU AT ALL.

Here is the scary thing when people point this out. "Hey, you have this blown-up balloon that looks like you, talks like you, and is kind of living a crazy life, but isn't you" – you might just say, "Oh yeah, F-Off!" Because well, that is a little embarrassing, and no one wants to cop up to that.

So, put all shame aside, if you want to feel the joy of being yourself. Just know we – ALL 100% – everyone is conditioned in this world to live as their NOT-SELF. No one I have witnessed, no matter how awake, evolved, spiritual, or how much work they have done on themselves, has avoided this conditioning experience.

So, no worries, let's laugh at it and try to let it go together. So, please take a deep breath with me here as we begin this profound journey together. Try and allow yourself to explore one Center per week. Spend time contemplating and engaging in the meditations (if, of course, only if this feels correct for you). Once you Decondition from the absorption of the world onto your Undefined Centers, you can awaken into your supersonic genius. Yes, each of the Undefined Centers holds deep wisdom and profound power once mastered.

As we go through each of the 9 Centers, I will be doing meditation after each Center. You can read this over and then repeat it back in your mind as you close your eyes, or record yourself saying them and then listen.

Or you can listen to the meditations we have created for you.

Check the PDF for where to find these.

The Head Center

Alright, so the very top triangle pointing up is the Head. The Head Center when it is Undefined is super tricky.

This Center is what is known as a pressure Center. This means you feel a ton of pressure to take action on all your thoughts, no matter how crazy they may be. Your mind tells you that you must do the things it THINKS you should do because...

Your parents want you to
It will mean you will be rich if you do
It will make you popular
It will create significant gains
If you don't, you will fail
If you don't, you will lose everything, your family, your house, your sanity, or even your life (yes, the mind can be that manipulative to get you to do things)
If you don't, you will be disliked

And my friend, you and I both know this list can go on and on and on. The Head pressure to act on thoughts is an endless monkey trap of the most insane kind.

The Head represents the mind, your thinking, your thoughts, it is absorbing and amplifying all of the world's thoughts, and it thinks these are all "my" thoughts. Then you feel pressure to act on these thoughts, turn these thoughts into a reality.

The thoughts keep coming, and they keep telling you what to think, and you have pressure to tell everyone what you are thinking about. Then you might want to say to the world (like on Facebook/Twitter/or at the dinner table) how important your thoughts are, and that everyone should think like you, or detail what other people should think. Oh, come on, you know you have done this.

Now, if you are entirely Open here, you just might feel so overwhelmed with all the thoughts coming in that you just don't know how to process them. You will abdicate all of your thinking to someone else.

Just think of a cult or religion, your priest, a guru, or even a husband or wife who gives their power of thought to someone else to think for them. There might be this sense: I don't know what to think, so *you* just think for me. Tell me what to think, what is right, what is moral, how to behave, what to believe. You do it for me because I just can't sort through all this mad pressure on my own. The thoughts will also tell you that you have such a good idea, you better go out and make it happen. Think of something you may have thought was a good idea, like starting a business, creating an invention. You are told by the general self-help or community at large, just go for it! Then you initiate miserably without your proper strategy and get incredibly angry, disappointed, bitter, or frustrated. Does anyone relate to this?

Here are some questions to answer if you have an Undefined (white) Head Center:

1. Am I trying to prove to the world what I think is essential?
2. Am I acting out on the pressures my mind is barking at me?
3. Am I overwhelmed with doubt or confusion?
4. Am I trying to know the unknowable?

How the Not-Self Mind might speak to those with an Undefined Head Center:

1. I need to look to who has the answer to all my questions; I need the solution.

2. I need a stimulating idea; if I go there, I will get answers and inspirations.
3. I am not sure how to think about this; where can I go to know how to think about this situation?
4. I think I know what to do; I have to take action on all my thoughts.
5. Pressure to contemplate many things that do not matter, answering questions that don't matter.

Aligned and clear state for this Undefined Head is to be able to witness the mind but not to be pressured to take action on thought. Knows which thought or inspiration is worthy and releases the need to chase, prove, or manifest ideas without listening to IA.

Aligned and clear state for a Defined Head (colored in) is to amplify inspiration, positivity, clarity of thought out to the world.

Defined Head expressing itself in a distorted frequency or unhealthy way: If you are Defined, and you are putting pressure on others to think as you do, or putting pressure on yourself with severe doubt, anxiety, or confusion, you may be misusing the Defined Head. In others words, you might overthink with pressure and stress. Do you think your thoughts are the best and should be pushed onto others as truth? Think again!

Watch for those with a Defined Head. If you are Undefined, pay attention to whether you are absorbing their thoughts, or if they are your own. Discover the Undefined/Defined Heads in your Inner Circle and witness how they operate this week. Did you have any amazing AHAs?

Meditation for the Undefined Head

This is a guided meditation for the Undefined Head. You can gently contemplate these words as you read. After you read through this, you can then guide yourself on the journey, record this and listen to it, or get the recorded versions on the PDF, https://foxy5d.com/pages/are-you-a-mutant, which also comes with the meditation for the Defined Head.

Breathe in, drop into the body, into feeling the weight of your body wherever you are sitting. Close all of your screens, shut your door, close Facebook, your phone, and tell your family this is time for you. Create a beautiful environment, light a candle, or perhaps turn on a beautiful light or grab a crystal. Create this as your sacred space; we will be going through each Center, so you will want this to be a blessed time.

For the Undefined Head: Let's just be still for a moment, feel into the body, breathe in with me here. Feel the breath expand and move through your body. Ask yourself, what thoughts are running you? Do you ruminate over thoughts that are not important? What thoughts run through your head all day? Are you trying to figure out how to make something happen? Are you questioning the possibility of everything? Do you doubt the people in your life? Is your mind overly active? Just notice if there is truth to any of these questions. Feel what it might feel like to allow the mind to relax for a moment.

Notice if you can imagine the mind taking the back seat and witnessing, rather than speaking and forcing the body to act, move, make decisions based on thoughts. How would that feel? How does it feel to witness? Do you notice ease in the body, less tension?

When you witness, can you let the epiphanies come? The epiphany will not come in the confusion or the thought it can come in the stillness.

An Undefined Head may get lost in the confusion, the swirling of thoughts. Perhaps these thoughts are not yours. Ask yourself, are these thoughts mine? What is it like to simply watch them?

The mind has its place; it can think, read, contemplate, even share thoughts with others when invited. But if it is the enslaver leading the body, making decisions, and forcing action, it might lead the whole life experience towards pain.

So, allow the mind for once to sit back and enjoy the ride.

The Ajna

The Head and the Ajna in this Human Design system are very much related. The distinction is what you might find in the difference between thoughts and ideas. There is a difference there, but it is hard to tease apart. The Ajna is similar, might be more correlated to the third eye in the Chakra system, where the Head Center is more like the Crown Chakra.

In Human Design, we understand this Center to be where ideas, as well as anxieties, are located. After a thought enters the Head Center, it then moves to the Ajna for the thought process. This would be where you find your credo, code of conduct, ideology, racism, judgments, opinions, choosing the right thought, or the wrong thought, ruminating on thoughts, and of course, demanding your thought is the best thought.

The Ajna connects the Head Center to the Throat. The thought comes into the Head, conceptualizes into an idea in the Ajna, and is voiced in the Throat.

Most of society has been trained to believe the mind and the intellect are the ruling force of the world. This mind that brought us up from cave dwellers and led us to be the creators that have conquered the earth is a force to revere. We love intelligent people; we still believe universities are the most coveted institutions on the planet for learning when they have not progressed in 30 years. The universities are stuck in the dark ages with little out-of-the-box thinking allowed (before you PhDs out there come for me – of course, there are exceptions).

The mind is the "GOD" we've been praying to for the last 411 years; we are all stuck there.

This intel is here to tell you – the mind is not horrible, but LISTEN UP, PEOPLE, it is not the thing to rely on anymore. It is not something to revere in another person anymore. It is time to realize this mind has some major, and I mean significant, limitations, as well as some pretty big toxic dark sides to it.

We have all come to think of this mind as more important than God (in many Western materialist societies, well this and the dollar). The mind is the most giant trap in today's world that there is.

The mind thinks it is in control; the mind thinks it has all the answers; the mind thinks it is so smart, clever, and can figure everything out. But unfortunately, when the mind is wrong or insecure, it gets super angry, causes fights and wars, and has to prove itself. If the mind is in anxiety, it goes for drugs; it hoards, it drinks itself to oblivion; it fucks, it snorts, it destroys the earth and anything in its path. It's a pretty dark, destructive, brutal-to-please force on the planet. If you are trying to stop an addiction, what is the mind telling you? "Don't worry about it, it's OK, there are worse things, you can do it, you deserve it." The mind is forcing some of the worst behaviors we do.

Also, if the mind's beliefs are questioned, it will kill the outside entity questioning it. Hence why so many heretics have been stoned, murdered, jailed for simply believing in something that does not fit the modern-day paradigm. Today you just get canceled on social media, ostracized, etc.

So, don't you think it's time to find a new way?

A sobering thought, isn't it. So, before you go and think, oh, come on, Raquel, my mind isn't that bad, I don't think horrible things; it is just everyone else's mind – THINK AGAIN. If you look inside and say, nope, my mind isn't talking, that is just me up there, you are so lost in your mind you can't separate out of it.

Everyone misuses the mind. If you notice, the mind is not a place for anyone to make a decision in Human Design. The Mental Inner Authority is shown on the Inner Authority as NONE so you are not to confuse the mind with being an authority. The mind is not to be used as a decision-making entity for anyone.

The mind can be used as an Outer Authority. The Outer Authority is when the mind is speaking the knowledge that is one hundred percent represented as the reflection of the unique genius of the person speaking but for another person. The Outer Authority is when the voice of the mind conveys, when invited or responding, information to assist the other. It is a perfect self-reflection, almost how you might imagine an enlightened master may speak. Let us just say this is rare. Very, very rare! There is much Deconditioning to take place for all of us to live up to this. Most of the time, the mind is a beautiful reflection of the NOT-SELF. I am no exception to this insidious issue. We, as humans, all face this all the time.

This Ajna is the Center for all this pain of the mind and anxiety. The Ajna takes on pressure of the head to conceptualize thoughts, take action on these thoughts, ruminate on the anxiety, and then speak our ideas to anyone who will listen or force it on those who will not. LOL!

Here are some questions to answer if you have an Undefined (white) Ajna:

1. Do I try to prove my point? Am I afraid to say I don't know?
2. Do I even really know what my point is?
3. Is anyone asking to hear my ideas?
4. Am I anxious? Is there rolling anxiety about life, business, a relationship that I ruminate over?

How the Not-Self Mind might speak to those with an Undefined Ajna Center (voice in the head):

1. I am certain that _____ (fill in the blank), and I need to let everyone know about my conviction.
2. I have to get my life together; I have to do something to

handle the chaos.

3. I have to figure out my life, what to do, I have to figure something out.
4. I have to show how certain I am; I have to prove my point to the world.

Aligned and clear state for this Undefined Ajna is to surrender and be comfortable in the not knowing. You might not have an answer, an idea, or you might not know the truth, so get comfortable with that.

Aligned and clear state for a Defined Head is to be comfortable with what you know, become a beacon for inspired ideas, but also be willing to hear other people's perspectives. Other people's ideas and opinions have value, and most importantly, everyone has a unique perspective. The faster you can come up to speed with allowing others their own unique perspectives, the faster we can finally heal this chaotic human soup we are all in.

Defined Ajna expressing itself in a distorted frequency or unhealthy way: If you are Defined, and you believe your idea is the only idea, think again. Try not to force onto others that your opinion is the only one. Look, I know this is hard for you. But everyone has the right to their concept. Don't worry; I still love you!

Meditation for the Undefined Ajna
Healing anxiety.

The mental anxiety of the world can linger here, this is incredibly uncomfortable, so in this meditation, we are actively going to soothe the anxiety in the mind.

Take a breath in with me, and for this meditation, bring a notepad and pen into the meditation area and take notes as we contemplate the following questions.

What anxieties plague you? Are you feeling the need to share your opinions? Do you think no one listens to your ideas or opinions? Do you feel pressure to voice your ideas? Do your ideas seem freak to you, and you fear you will be ridiculed? In general, ask yourself, what thoughts bring you feelings of anxiety?

Is it possible to be in the not knowing?

How does it feel to release the pressure of trying to prove your point? How does it feel to question what is happening rather than trying to explain what is happening?

A good mantra: the universe shows me the way, allows me to see more significant aspects of learning, or self, when I become comfortable in the uncertainty.

Let me align to what is wanting to come through my life rather than forcing my ideas onto my life.

I am willing to let go of my ideas and opinions and open the door for new ideas.

I let the ideas come through; I ask if these are mine. If these are vibrating at the highest frequency of love, do these ideas feel positive? I will not act on these ideas; I will follow my Inner Authority. However, I witness the ideas and honor them. As I witness the anxiety, I can feel a sense of peace moving through my body. Feel the body, notice the beauty and transformation of the infinite intelligence available in the vehicle intelligence. It is the intelligence beyond the mind.

The Throat Center

All the energy of the Circuits is moving towards the Throat Center. The force is coming down from the Head Center and moving up from the Root Center, all aiming to reach the Throat. The Head and the Root are pressure Centers. So you can imagine this force drives humans to speak, do, make shizz happen, manifest stuff, talk a lot, and usually, this is done from conditioning force and outside influences. But the energy is all trying to get to the Throat. So, what does this mean? We are all trying to express the energy we have going through our systems. The Throat is, you guessed it, the Center for communication. It also represents the manifestation of bringing thought into form. There is a lot of power and complexity around the Throat Center.

So let me wrap this up by saying – humans are pressure centers forced to make things happen by crazy thoughts, insecurities, and fears that aren't yours. So, you wonder why people look so nuts out there? Well, there you have it crisply condensed in one sentence.

The first thing to note is that Human Design teaches this very differently from any other spiritual teaching about the Throat, and if you can get this, it just might change all of the "manifesting" in your life. So, the first thing to note is that no one is designed to tell anyone *what to do*. The energy of the Throat is designed to express the Channel or Gate off the Throat. Either To INFORM for Manifestors (this is as if there is a motor directly to the Throat), informing, as you now know, is to inform others about what you are about to do; it does not mean *tell others what they should do*. Or this energy is in RESPONSE; if your Channel reaches the Sacral, then it would be a Generated Channel. For many, the definition off the Throat is from a Projected Channel, which means that all good ideas, thoughts, and manifestations should come after recognition. Yes, this is true even for Types that are not Projectors. FYI, most opinions fall in this category.

Responding means, you don't start a conversation; you wait to have something to react to. Or, it would help if you waited until recognized to share any ideas, thoughts, opinions, or what you are about to do. Any words used to force anyone to do anything, manipulate another person, tell someone what they should do, or even share before they are supposed to is just chaotic noise at best, abuse at worst. For the most part, 90% of the population has no understanding of this at all, and all the communications and speaking opinions and forcing things to happen are entirely out of alignment with how this Center operates. We see the world adhering to pressure to share what they think, demand others think like them, or having an intolerance for any differing of opinion. Most people are not listening to any ideas that threaten the foundation of their belief system (i.e., religious isolation), ranting about their ideas, sharing with people that have no space for the answer (before being asked). Most people are not adhering to this philosophy of how this Center was designed to operate. This is why there is so much noise out there in the world. Many people talk, spew opinions and ideas with religious fervor, and it is super common for everyone to tell people what to do and think. Do you ever notice this, or is it just me?

If you are a Projector with a Defined Throat, you have more consistent access to how you will communicate, but you still need to wait to be invited before speaking.

Here are some questions to answer if you have an Undefined (white) Throat:

1. Am I desperately trying to be heard?
2. Am I trying to get attention?
3. Are my ideas, opinions, insights honored and invited, or ignored?

How the Not-Self might speak to those with an Undefined Throat Center:

1. What can I do to get attention? Is anyone noticing me or liking my posts/pics/videos, or responding to me?
2. What do I have to do to manifest? I have to manifest this thing now.
3. Why isn't anyone talking? This silence is killing me; what can I say to fill the gap in conversation?

Aligned and clear state for this Undefined Throat: I know I have important things to say and can impact many people with my words when I am first recognized or invited to share my ideas.

A naturally healthy state for a Defined Throat: I use my Strategy and Inner Authority for the right timing and trust my words affect those people who need my tonal frequency.

Defined Throat expressing itself in a distorted frequency or unhealthy way: Speaking over other people; aggressive with words; expressing loaded ideas as ultimate truth. Pressuring others to manifest or speak when it might not be correct for them.

Meditation for the Undefined Throat

Come into a place of stillness and quiet. The Undefined Throat longs to use its superpower of the voice to be understood by many different people. So, let's explore how to use this properly. Breathe in, breathe out, feel the body, feel into the power of the Throat.

The Throat is a robust Center of communication and manifestation. We all want to be heard, seen, and understood, but as we realize in Human Design, this is best done when we are operating correctly as our unique selves.

Feeling into this Center, it is imperative to become aware that there is a shadow here and a superpower. The shadow side of this Center is activated when you are desperate to be heard when you try and speak, but no one is listening or understands your genius. If this happens and you continue to talk, you might suffer. If you can learn to wait to be invited and notice who wants to know your wisdom before speaking, many blessings and magic can come from your voice.

Of course, this depends on the rest of your chart. If you are a Generator, you will need to respond, and if you are Projector, you will need to wait a little longer until you are fully recognized as yourself.

Feel into the power of communication; when it is the right timing for the right people, you just allow your truth to come out. You don't need the mind to get involved or overly intellectualize what you will say; you just let your truth soar. You may feel gun-shy to speak since your genius has been so often ignored and unseen; maybe someone stole your beautiful ideas in the past. So the healing can happen once you know that waiting is the key. Once you do this, many people will be inspired, turned on, and excited about your words. Those people who need to hear what you have to say will listen to you and be inspired by your truth. This empowers your voice and allows your superpower to become ignited. Feel the relaxation when your Throat is operating correctly. Relax, allow, let others ask for your knowledge.

The G-Center

The G-Center is another Center that is unique to Human Design. The 7-Centered beings, according to Ra Uru Hu, have different ways of operating than the 9-Centered being.

According to Ra Uru Hu, he felt that the information from this system was like an operating manual for this more evolved being.

Interestingly enough, we are evolving again in 2027, which means we need to understand how the nine Centers operate so we can easily and gracefully move into our next level of evolution.

So, even though these Centers are similar to the Chakra System, they operate very differently, and there isn't an equivalent to this Center. This G-Center is the Center of identity, knowing who you are and what you are here to do. The Magnetic Monopole here pulls the Unconscious (Design) side together with the Conscious or the Personality side into one coherent expression of life.

This Center here is all about love and direction, and it assists us in knowing WHO WE ARE. This Center is almost like water for a fish for the people who are defined – it just is. And you just are who you are. Please note many people who are Defined relate to the Undefined aspects. This is because even Defined people struggle with understanding their place in the world, who they are, and trying to fit in. It's just that the Undefined absorb and amplify this to the point of literally becoming the people they are with, wholly losing themselves in the mix.

It can be a little or a lot more challenging for those Undefined people, so let's explore some more profound questions for them.

Here are some questions to answer if you have an Undefined (white) G-Center:

1. Do I search for love, meaning, in all the wrong places?
2. Am I desperate to understand my direction or who I am going to be when I grow up?
3. Do I struggle to know who I am, or what niche my business should be?

How the Not-Self might speak to those with an Undefined G-Center:

1. I'm lost; who loves me? Where should I look for my next partner? Let's go there.
2. What should I do with my life? Who am I? Who can tell me?
3. I have to find the right career/business niche, but where? How? Who can direct me?

Aligned and clear state for this Undefined G-Center: I know I can easily fit into many environments, I am not going to force myself to be a certain way.

Aligned and clear state for a Defined G-Center: I am comfortable with who I am, but I don't force others to tell me who they are or demand they know their direction. (Particularly for parents with children with an Undefined G-Center.) I don't force people to discover a specific niche, career or identity Is an excellent mantra.

Defined G-Center expressing itself in a distorted frequency or unhealthy way: Demanding that others know what they want to be when they grow up, forcing them into specific niches in life or business.

Meditation for the Undefined G-Center

Take a moment to relax and center yourself. There is chameleon-like energy here when you are Undefined G. This fluidity is a beautiful gift. Honor your abilities to move in and out of environments; see your strength with this. Even though you can fit in and adapt, this is not who you are, so don't define yourself. You don't need to determine who you are; surrender to being comfortable with being malleable with not knowing. Being able to fit in anywhere is your gift, so allow the fluidity.

Imagine yourself so beautifully becoming the world around you. If you walk into a room of leaders, they see you as one of them. If you are in a bar, you fit in. You belong wherever you are. This begs the question, are you in the right environment with the right people? As you can imagine, this is imperative for you. Using your particular Inner Authority will help you. If you are getting a no, leave that location.

Morphing into groups is a fantastic superpower gift; you never need to define yourself, just be in awe of all the places you fit in. Allow yourself not to feel the pressure to have to define yourself. If you are on an endless search to find yourself, to find love, just let that go for a moment and release the question. Notice which environments you feel best in. Now be willing to honor yourself if you are with the wrong people. If your house feels wrong, this is a huge red flag you need to move on. Which room do you love, which restaurant makes you feel fabulous? Being in the right environment is so crucial, so feel into places that inspire you. Which chair in your home is your favorite? Contemplate how you can make your domain more aligned with your joy.

The Ego Center

The Ego/Will/Heart Center (referred to as all three things): This is another Center that is very different in Human Design than in the Chakra system. In Human Design, we begin to realize that looking at these Centers through the Undefined (white) and Defined (colored in) gives us an entirely new way to comprehend these Centers. There is not one person I have spoken with who didn't relate to the qualities of being Defined or Undefined when I introduce these concepts to them. Yet, no other system looks at these Centers with this insight, so in other words, contemplating these Centers can relieve a lot of pain and suffering in your life.

For me, contemplating where I was Defined, which also means where I have a consistent way of understanding the energy in the specific Center, completely reorganized my understanding of life. Powerfully for the first time, it was as though I was given a pair of proper reading glasses; I COULD SEE CLEARLY in how I operated in the world.

Most definitely, in the Undefined Centers, there is an inconsistency you might absorb and amplify the most exaggerated aspects of the Center, particularly if you are not aware of Human Design. The Undefined Will is one of the most challenging Centers in the entire system. Contemplating how this operates will support you in such earth-shattering ways; just trust me. If you are Undefined, spend some time going through these concepts slowly.

The Ego Center is the Center for business, self-esteem, and willpower.

When Undefined, you just might have trouble with them all. Charging your worth, motivating to get things done, overcommitting but not having the wherewithal to follow through. Not feeling valuable enough to ask for a raise or charge your worth, these are all issues you might see with this Undefined Center. Most people with this Undefined Center feel this monkey on their back starting from being young children. Those with an Undefined Will are incredibly sensitive to sharp criticism by parents when they are young; the wound runs far deeper for them.

The entire self-improvement/motivational industry centers around this Center. There is societal pressure to self-improve every area of your life. Be sexier, prettier, more intelligent, more affluent, get a bigger house, a better body, and whatever you do, do not see the inherent value in you just being you.

This distortion, of course, comes from those with a Defined Ego, overinflating their self-esteem/ego prowess. Over the years, I've witnessed high dysfunction here in the heart; the Defined Will is pumping their self-worth to the point of pain and exhaustion. Meaning this distorted defined Ego turns into full-fledged "narcissism," for lack of a better term. They might just feel so special, always demanding the need to prove worth to everyone around them and taking up the breath in the room at all times. Fighting for the top spot of the have or the have-not's food chain. Remember, I am from Los Angeles, where just maybe this Ego thing is more cartoonish than anywhere else in the world.

This overinflated and distorted sense of self-worth is one of the most painful existences you can have as a human; all about the ME equates to a life of severe suffering. Those with this Defined, are constantly battling this pressure to learn the humility of a healthy Ego.

Understanding how this Undefined and Defined Center can be healthy or unhealthy resolves much of humanity's suffering.

So feel into the journey of healing the Ego.

Here are some questions to answer if you have an Undefined (white) Ego Center:

1. Do I commit to things I know I shouldn't?
2. Do I criticize myself or everything I do – after the fact?
3. Do I undervalue my work, my business, myself?

How the Not-Self might speak to those with an Undefined Ego Center:

1. I have to prove to people I am valuable, so I better say I will do what they want me to do.
2. I have to commit to that event, work deadline, anything to prove my worth.
3. I have to be better, I am not good enough at work, as a wife, as a boss/employee, I need to make them believe I'm enough.
4. I have to tell everyone I am better than I am, put on a heroic face, be in control even though on the inside I feel worthless.

Aligned and clear state for this Undefined Ego: I know that I am inherently valuable just by being myself; I don't need to overcommit. I trust a more significant source, THY WILL, and I follow my Strategy and Inner Authority for the right action.

Aligned and clear state for a Defined Ego: I don't pressure people to do things, pump up their egos with the "COME ON, YOU CAN DO IT" attitude. I am aware of where I pressure others to commit; I am aware of when I have an overinflated value over other people.

Defined Ego/Will/Heart expressing itself in a distorted frequency or unhealthy way: Forcing others to feel as self-assured as they do, hyper motivation pushing others in all the wrong directions. Feeling they are in some way superior due to accomplishments over other people. The distorted unhealthy Defined Ego will walk with a superiority complex that sounds like: I am better than you because I am richer, skinnier, more beautiful, more successful, I have a family, I accomplished a goal, I am talented, I have a higher place in society, I have more followers, and this list could go on and on. Together awareness can heal this Center. So, let's do this together in the below meditation.

Meditation for the Undefined Ego Center

Close your eyes, feel into the powerful force of your will. Allow your body to relax and surrender to the sweetness of the love of the heart. This tender heart is a place where you feel love, gratitude, appreciation. This is the Center for willpower, for business, for the heart. Your Undefined Will Center might feel like the monkey on your back always telling you that you just didn't rise-up to the occasion. This is that little voice inside you after you do a video, or you go live, or even after you speak at the dinner table that says, "That was the stupidest thing to say, how could you say that, you should never have mentioned that."

It is the place inside that will tell you not to take a risk. It will say to you after you took a chance and had an awful experience, why you should never assume that risk again. It is the place inside you that tells you why you will fail at diets, why you will never succeed, so don't try. This place inside will also want to overcommit to things you know you will just never accomplish but saying you will do it momentarily satisfies something in you that later makes you feel bad about yourself for not following through.

So, feel into this broken heart, this place of wounded self-esteem, and for one moment, just know these thoughts are NOT YOU.

Your heart and your will are perfectly aligned when you wait for energy based on your Strategy and Inner Authority. So, feel what it feels like to be motivated from an entirely different place. Don't let the mind take over and tell you that you are not good; or on the flip side, it will overinflate your worth. Neither is true. You are simply a perfect reflection of the divine perfection just as you are.

Neither better nor worse than anyone else. So, surrender your will to thy will, the higher will, and let the mind surrender to no mind. You align with Strategy and Inner Authority within this place, and so much energy aligns in the right direction. You are beautiful, perfect, you are amazing just as you are. You are here for a reason; you are here to fulfill your magical piece to the universal puzzle with your perfection. Relax, you are exactly where you should be, your life is aligned, you are valuable, I see your genius, now claim your unique genius for yourself. No one can be you; this is a mystical statement. Feel the power in it.

Solar Plexus/Emotional Center

This area in the chart is also known as the Emotional Center. The Solar Plexus is the place where all the emotions reside. This Center is so powerful that it becomes the Inner Authority when colored in (Defined) for any Type. So, imagine that when Emotions are defined, they control the entire decision-making process; this Center trumps all other Centers. It is the monster in the IA hierarchy. And you know what, who doesn't intuitively get this. We would all say, oh yup, those emotions, the super juicy highs are incredible, and when the low depressions hit, there is nothing worse.

Emotions are friggin intense. I feel like if the Universe or the collective consciousness just understood the Emotions from the Human Design perspective, we would awaken as a whole.

It is important to note that the Defined Emotional being has been powerfully controlled and suppressed by the Undefined

Emotional beings because the Undefined Emotionals just can't handle how intense the emotions are. However, if they understood they were just absorbing and amplifying the feelings of the other and knew how to transcend this, they wouldn't be so unbelievably uncomfortable in their skin. All antidepressants might disappear off the planet in one clean sweep.

OK, that is an exaggeration. Big Pharma, don't come for me!

It is also important to note, and this might be a shocker to the world, the Emotional side of the Human Design chart is also more masculine. The Feminine is intuitive, in the moment, and non-emotional (when, of course, the Emotional Being appropriately expresses their feelings). HMMM, head-scratcher? How did this get turned so upside-down? Also, note that just because it is masculine, it does not mean male. These Aura Mechanics exist in both men/women/transgender/androgynous/gay/straight/everyone. I have seen so many people define feminine and masculine traits as the feminine being deeply in flow with the emotions, which is not true. The fierce archetypal tribal feminine in Human Design is the provider of the values of the tribe clearly, directly, and without emotional waves that are theirs.

One thing to contemplate is that any male without the Emotional Center defined who is deeply uncomfortable with an Emotional man may have aggressively repressed these emotional waves. I am not blaming men, but it's important to note that this entire wave is so uncomfortable that we have collectively ushered it onto the women as the cause, and ruthlessly tried to cut it off from both men and women and all people alike. The freeing of feelings for all Emotional beings of any gender would be a rarified space of healing for those brave enough to do so.

Emotional beings should be deep, feeling everything and safely but thoroughly expressing their emotions. Unfortunately, this simple how-to memo is lost to the world at large. Instead, most Emotional beings are so cut off, drugged, or heavily medicated, controlled, repressed, and forced to make rash decisions on emotional swings because no one has the patience to give them time and space to feel it out first. This situation has caused emotional chaos in the world. The Undefined Emotional beings act out these repressed emotions like wild broncos with no control. So, just to reiterate, the Undefined Emotional being is absorbing, amplifying, and radically distorting the emotions of the Defined Emotional being who is most likely severely repressed emotionally. They are addicted to the drama, without any awareness that these emotions are not even theirs. I know, I just solved the world's problems with one sentence.

But, seriously, I spent an entire two years (not to mention the decade of therapy following my degree) in a room taking on the emotions of everyone around me when I was earning my Master's Degree. I would cry the minute I walked into the space; people were healing deep trauma, wounds from childhood, and physical as well as sexual abuse. The processing was profound, and although it helped me immensely with some past trauma, I also processed 200 people's unhealed emotional stuff. I had some past wounds and issues, but nothing like what I witnessed. Because I had not yet been introduced to how these Defined and Undefined Centers operate, I would take on the emotional intensity of the class and spent years processing it. Nothing cleared my emotional pain like Human Design. Much less of the endless processing was necessary after I learned I was Undefined. I finally felt calm emotionally for the first time in my life. Now, yes, it did take some Deconditioning, but very quickly, I began to feel relief. I suffered a lifetime of extreme emotions, nervous anxiety, highs, and lows; I would do anything to calm them down. Today, I have an emotional stillness I would never have imagined possible; it is incredibly soothing and enjoyable. I will note that for anyone who has trauma and those who are Emotional, and really for everyone, doing therapy is incredibly important. However, if we just integrated the uniqueness of each person, wow, talk about game-changing. Those people brave enough to incorporate these Human Design teachings into their therapy or Spiritual Psychology will serve people on a far grander scale.

This Emotional ride is very intense whether you are Defined or Undefined, so let's explore the wave together. Grab your surfboard, jump in, the water is warm!

Here are some questions to answer if you have an Undefined (white) Solar Plexus:

1. Is what I am feeling mine?
2. Am I willing to observe and not absorb the emotions I feel?
3. If someone erupts in my home, office, or anywhere, emotionally, is it possible to not take it personally, simply witness, and allow others to feel it?

How the Not-Self might speak to those with an Undefined Solar Plexus Center:

1. I am afraid to express my opinion or truth on the matter because I don't want to insult anyone. I am going to avoid the conflict then usually there is an explosion.
2. I feel uncomfortable talking about this topic, so I am going just to avoid it altogether.
3. I don't want to see that person or be in that situation because it makes me uncomfortable. Or the flip side is, I need some type of drama or stimulation to feel alive – so I will ruminate on this dramatic situation that happened yesterday/two years ago/ten years ago. Or I will instigate a drama.
4. I have to ghost that person or cut them out because I can't handle the pain. (This is not a healthy person's reaction unless, of course, you are dealing with any type

of abuse, including narcissistic abuse, and sometimes cutting off is the ONLY answer.)

Aligned and clear state for this Undefined Solar Plexus or the non-Emotional Being: I am calm and feel safe and aligned, these emotions and this drama are not mine. I am healthy and healed in my emotional understanding. It is safe to witness, allow energy to move through me, feel completely, relax, then release, and understand that naturally, my emotions are calm.

Aligned and clear state for a Defined Solar Plexus or the Emotional Being: I am comfortable feeling all my feelings. I will not let anyone push them down, including myself. I will not assign a story to my low wave; I am just low. I will use this low wave for creative expressions. I will not make decisions on a high wave or a downward wave. I will feel the depth and color of all my emotions.

Defined Solar Plexus expressing itself in a distorted frequency or unhealthy way: Stuffing down emotions to be completely removed emotionally, living in the mental realm. Blowing up when upset or emotionally projecting pain onto someone else. Passive-aggressive behavior. Unable to adequately express your emotions or extreme emotional outbursts.

Meditation for the Undefined Solar Plexus

Begin to feel, drop into the emotions. What type of emotions do you feel the most often? Do you remember if someone in your family growing up was always emotional? In other words, if you are depressed, ask yourself if anyone in your household growing up was depressed. Try for a moment just to feel everything and ask yourself, are these emotions mine? Try on the concept that maybe these emotions are not mine. Is it possible all the drama you are amplifying is simply an addiction to drama, and it is not you? Contemplate the role drama has played in your life. Do you try to create it?

Lean into this statement: I am allowing myself to be a screen, let it move through me. I will not be a sponge, and I will not absorb the pain of the world anymore. I feel into the emotions without pushing them away or holding onto emotions I love. I can be calm; I can witness and be simply in my joy, my satisfaction, my peace, and wonderment of life. I am allowed to let my vehicle lead the way in its infinite intelligence. I am so grateful to know that when intense emotions move through me, I don't need to attach a story. Usually, they are from someone in my environment. But if I do not know exactly, I don't need to know; I just need to witness.

There is power in the witness. There is power in rising up and witnessing the emotions. There is power in not being so emotional. Can you feel the calm in this? How beautiful it is just to allow these emotions, to watch as others explode. You don't need to push it down, control it, or take it on.

Calm, clear, centered is your natural state. Can you feel this? It is powerful to know and allow this truth to settle in.

Spleen

The Spleen is an immensely interesting Center because if you have studied any of the Chakra systems, you may not be familiar with this term. For those of you who are a Splenic Inner Authority, this Spleen is super important for you. Yet, you may not have heard this term before in any other spiritual teachings. So, the Spleen is not like any of the traditional spiritual Chakra Centers. Because it is a unique Center to this Human Design knowledge, it is so important to understand. Nowhere else are we taught to listen to the Spleen, and why it is also a little more challenging to understand. Also, please note that if you are Undefined here, this affects you deeply in your life and behavioral patterns. The Spleen (counter to the name) is not located in the Spleen or any one specific area in the body like the other Centers. The Spleen insight runs through the entire lymphatic system. It is like having little ears and eyes all over the body. It is felt like a movement happening before the actual thought comes in. The Spleen is super intuitive, but for me understanding the Spleen was utterly different from how the intuition was described to me in the past. So, even though I am Splenic Inner Authority and the Spleen is directly associated with intuition, when people would tell me to listen to my intuition, I thought intuition was a clear voice or directive in my head. It always threw me off dramatically when I followed this. So, the Spleen is very different, and understanding how it operates will immensely help those who are Splenic. The Spleen is primitive in a way. It has a fight or flight type knowing of things that are healthy for you.

The Undefined Spleen works very differently from the Defined Spleen as, of course, do all the Centers. Undefined Spleen people have the possibility of not feeling so good in general; they have a sensitive immune system and might feel sick more than most people until they learn how to use this Center properly.

That includes learning how to not hold onto things past their expiration date that are unhealthy for them. This need to release stuff is with things and with relationships, homes, careers, anything that you need to move on from, but you might feel this uncanny desire to hold on even if you know it is super toxic for you. The more you can let go of these things, the better, and the more likely you will feel free and healthy.

The Spleen is a Center for health, psychic knowing, and survival. It operates in the now – like supersonic ears knowing what to jump for or leap out of the way of, long before your mind can tell you.

The trick is not letting the thoughts disrupt the Splenic awareness and leave you doubting your Spleen. So, in other words, the Splenic awareness knows things long before your intellect can determine. Our society has relied on brainpower for answers, and the intellectual sword of severity cuts down all your Splenic knowing as unreliable, as stupid, or as things you can't prove. Over time, most people are conditioned not to trust this incredibly brilliant yet somewhat hard to hear genius.

Here are some questions to answer if you have an Undefined (white) Spleen:

1. Am I attached to my stuff?
2. Am I in a career, relationship, home past the expiration date?
3. Do I know I need to let go or move on, and yet still I am attached?
4. Am I afraid of things in a panic or anxiety?

How the Not-Self might speak to those with an Undefined Spleen Center:

1. I am afraid I don't know enough; I have to know more.
2. I can't let go of that stuff or that person, I am fearful of being alone without my comforts.
3. I am scared of repeating the past mistakes if I make that move (this can relate to house, job, career, person), so I will stay where I am.
4. I have to do that perfectly, or I will fail.
5. I don't feel good; what can I do to make myself feel better? (I.e. buy things, needy for people.)

Aligned and clear state for this Undefined Spleen: I am willing to release that which no longer serves me. A superpower is available for your health, security, fear, attachment when you pay attention to where you have gripped onto things for the comfort you know you should release. You can free yourself from fear when you let go of the anxiety that is not yours. A good mantra: I am not afraid to release things; I am willing to sense what is healthy for me.

Aligned and clear state for a Defined Spleen: I listen to the subtle whisper, and I listen to my intuition which is wisdom beyond and before my mind.

I will sense what fear is and what is my Inner Authority. I know the difference, and I take courageous action rather than letting fear stop me. I hear my Spleen, and I align to health by listening to my intuitive knowing. I do not push what is healthy for me onto other people.

Defined Spleen expressing itself in a distorted frequency or unhealthy way: The Defined Spleen that does not listen to itself will follow the mind telling it what to do. It doesn't trust intuition, and it ignores the whispers and only listens to the mind chatter for direction. You pressure others to do what you think is healthy for them.

Meditation for the Undefined Spleen

Slow down, take a breath in, and let's settle into wellness together. Feel into the fears and anxieties that might be gripping you. For one moment, just let those fears speak to you. Let any anxiety come forward. What are you afraid of? Do you have things in your life you know you need to let go of but feel too attached to? Is there stuff in your corners, drawers, the garage that need to be thrown away? Is there some wisdom you can gather from your body guiding you to things that are healthy for you? Just listen in for a moment.

Do you have a relationship that is not serving you? Are you in a career you would like to leave? Just allow this feeling to come forward; you don't need to take any action. Just be willing to release the cords or strings of attachment to things that no longer serve you and see if you feel lighter.

The next area of contemplation is your health. Are you feeling a general sense of well-being? Are you uncomfortable, or do you feel you can do things to assist your health or immune system? Let the answers come forward in awareness in your body. When aligned with things that are healthy for you and you naturally release the toxic situations and people, you can then awaken a superpower that aligns to a healthier life and maybe even notices what is healthy for others. Try and align to feeling good inside. This can turn into your supersonic knowing by touching the health and well-being of others. So, allow yourself to feel good, be willing to let go, know what is healthy, what to hold onto, and how to align to health. Once you allow this to flow through you, you will become wise here.

Root

The Root is a pressure Center, like the Head, and let me tell you: there is a lot of pressure here. This energy is the pressure to get shizz done. This Center is a pulse, so there is energy or not. The idea here is not to push when there is no energy. However, this is not how we have been trained to live or to work. So, for the most part, the majority of humanity is probably taking a shot of espresso with the motto, energy or not – I'm getting this shizz done. So, needless to say, most people are not following this properly.

What that is saying is that if there is no energy and you do something anyway, you slowly begin the process of burning out. As you all know, burnout leads to all types of stress and illness in the body, and hence much of the sickness we witness is stress-related. Being run-down makes you far more susceptible to any disease, as well as a case of the career blues.

Those people who are Undefined here have an amplified sense of pressure to get something completed. However, they often never, even after finishing tasks, feel relief from this pressure. So, it is a driving force on the planet that usually drives people into a world of discomforts.

It drives people to do, to make things happen, to get, to build, to complete tasks, and for some people, this might be fine. For other people, this may have led them to a life that resembles a whole lot of caffeine-frazzled crazy monkeys fighting for the most giant banana.

It is not that we are not supposed to do things; it's just we are not supposed to do what others tell us to do or what the societal pressure is.

Just a little FYI, this pressure is so subtle and all-encompassing that it was super hard for me to spot it for years. When I finally realized it, I noticed it as a slight pressure to do everything faster. To eat fast or to complete a sentence in a rush when people were anxious, or hurrying at the supermarket, running to get home, scurrying around for no particular reason that I needed to be in such a hurry for. But, it was so ever-present for most of my life. It was indeed a while before the AHA came rushing in on this one, and like one big giant Dalí painting, my whole reality felt skewed instantaneously.

We are supposed to follow our own inner convictions and Inner Authority to guide our lives. Once we follow what is correct for us, we align to a new level of our own precious timing for life, and it is a whole new world.

So, pressure for the sake of pressure, putting stress on others to do things that aren't correct for them, is part of the toxicity on the planet. Hearing this news might challenge many or all bosses, teachers, parents, coaches, employers out there – sorry-not-sorry. I am sure many of them do not want to hear this because it challenges all of their systems.

Exactly why we are encouraging most of you to bust out of those systems and live a life that is correct for you.

Here are some questions to answer if you have an Undefined (white) Root:

1. Am I feeling pressure to get something done?
2. Is it possible for me to just witness this pressure and

only take action when it is aligned with my proper IA and Strategy?

3. Do I feel guilt, discomfort, or the need TO DO things driving me forward in life?

4. Am I willing to feel the pressure but notice if I act on it whether the stress goes away or not?

How the Not-Self might speak to those with an Undefined Root Center:

1. I have to get this done in a hurry.
2. I have to make something happen now, what is the next thing I can do?
3. Where is the next new experience?
4. I have to complete this task, I have to hurry to my next item on my "to do" list.
5. I have to achieve more now, I have to accomplish more now.

Aligned and clear state for this Undefined Root: I am moving at my own pace. I know that I want to complete tasks, mark things off my to-do list. I can feel that. However, if I don't have the energy, I am not going to do those things. I am going to wait for the right timing, the right pace. I notice when people put pressure on me, I feel it, acknowledge it. It can be uncomfortable, but I will not let it drive me into work for the sake of work. I am not going to let it push me to do anything. I notice the difference in motivation; I am willing to pay attention to this and let my own Inner Authority and conviction move me.

Aligned and clear state for a Defined Root: I move peacefully at my own pace. I honor when the pulse is available and when it is not. I notice the pulse and complete things when there is the drive to do so. I also will try not to put pressure on others to do something. I will be aware that my energy naturally puts pressure on others, so I am making people uncomfortable if I actively increase that pressure.

I will align to the correct pulse and allow others to align to their right pulse.

Defined Root expressing itself in a distorted frequency or unhealthy way: The Defined Root is an energy that can negatively affect those around them. Putting any type of time restraints, get this done by this time, or buy this quickly – all these tactics in business may have worked in the past but will not continue to work for you. Allow others the freedom of their process. This might be challenging for the parents or bosses but experiment with this notion. Humanity longs for freedom from this pressure. It is a healing force on the planet when you can allow this to operate correctly. Plus, ultimately, everyone will complete more accomplished work more successfully at the right time when this pressure is relieved.

Meditation for the Undefined Root

Take a breath in with me, settle in and relax. Can you notice that you have a challenge of constantly worrying about getting things done? Do you feel a force pressuring you to work harder? A sense you need to make more, do more, succeed more? Does this pressure ever cause you to get tasks done frantically? Running around perhaps in a frenzied manner rather than as an empowered leader, visionary, or just aligned calm, creative force in the world? This energy is so intense. It has been part of your conditioning since childhood, so it is natural to have taken this on, absorbing it and running with it.

However, it doesn't ever go away, so the more you do, the more TO DOs your boss, your teacher, your employer will give you. The more you do the more you have to do. This is uncomfortable. You work more, you work harder, but the pressure is never relieved.

For one moment, just let all that pressure fall off you and

seep into the earth. Just let it go the best you can. What does it feel like to release all the "to-dos" in your life? Or maybe just the pressure to make something of yourself, what if that was gone too? What does it feel like to just BE? To be still, in this moment, allowing the body to settle in, to relax, to enjoy being alive for no other reason but you are here now. Just allow this feeling, let your body start to feel alive because the breath is now fuller with less pressure. Let the breath expand, let the joy of life and living take over. Let the body feel in this moment the pure essence of exultation!

Is there a difference? Notice this and then watch how fast the mind will tell you to get back to the list, making it all happen, and this time you can just witness it. See the pressure. This is not that easy to do. You rise above most of the population on the planet when you step into the witness. It is an incredibly empowering place to be. So, feel this, honor this observation, let it sink in, notice how it makes your body relax, maybe for the first time in your life. Just let yourself relax. This is one of the most intense areas in the chart to be Undefined or Open (no hanging Gates at all). This pressure has been coming at you a hundred miles an hour since you were born and carted off to school. Unraveling this takes time and space, and patience. So, let yourself feel this moment; repeat this meditation as often as you need. Please pay attention to the pressure. For some of you, it might be so subtle, like the air we breathe. We are so used to it we do not even notice it. But the more you contemplate, observe, feel, are present, the more powerfully these Not-Self themes will make themselves known to you!

Sacral
Hold on, everyone, the Sacral is the power Center for the world. Get the seat belts in place; this is a wild ride! This Sacral is where the life force energy, sex, money, power, and work come from, this area here. If this is colored in, you are automatically

a Generator or a Manifesting Generator. For those of us white or Undefined here, you are either a Manifestor, Reflector, or a Projector. This Center has a significant impact on all of us; we will spend some time contemplating this Center.

The Sacral runs the world. It is the consistent life force energy to work, make money, have sex and make the babies. Lots of juicy life force fuel is located in this Center. We needed it to build the world over the last 400 years. Capitalism, the government, the banks, the cities, the hospitals, the universities, infrastructure of highways, all these things were built by Generator life force energy. The bargaining agreement we were in was, *"You work for me, and I will be nice to you; give you money, a pension, a 401k."* You might not like what you do, but it will be suitable for everyone. We ran like this for a long time; actually, most of society is still running like this. If you work for Corporate America, you know that the longer hours you put into the workplace, you are more revered.

So, this is a lot of pain for the Undefined, 30% of the population who just cannot keep up with this force. Also, as we spoke about often in this book, the old work bargain is just not going to support the self-actualization for anyone anymore. The Generator fuel is not going anywhere; it's just that this energy will be redirected not just to serve the tribe but to serve the self. So, this collapse how we work in the world, is inevitable. We have no idea what will happen, but we know that those lazy Projector, Undefined Sacrals are here to lead the way in this shift.

First order of business, we must stop the glorification of BUSY. I am from LA, and this seems almost impossible. The busier in LA, the more popular you are. If your phone is blowing up, you leave early or arrive late because you are so slammed with social opportunities, you are the queen/king of the land.

All of these dynamics are in dire need of change. After Deconditioning from this energy, the Undefined Sacral will demonstrate the power in taking naps, slowing down, doing less. It will show us that play, and joy, peace, and awe are essential. If you are tired, it is not the time to drink that second cup of coffee. NO!!! It is time to stop, drop, and get under the covers for a snooze, that is.

You do not have to keep up. The more rested you are, the less stressed you will feel, the more aligned your Aura will become, the more power you will experience. You will be able to accomplish a 12-hour day in three hours if you are rested. However, the conditioning around this is not to relax but to push harder and just take a few Adderall, no-doze, a couple of lines, Red Bull, or whatever you need to get through the day. You see, most Undefined Sacrals are absorbing the Generator fuel, believing it is them, amping it up, and appearing to work longer and harder than most Generators until they might suddenly pop-off. These Undefined Sacral beings are usually addicted to some kind of something. Then you cannot sleep, and the entire insomnia epidemic is generally based on this because you need need support and sleeping meds to fall asleep.

So, here we are for all of the Undefined Sacrals in the world. Imagine the global revolution you will stir if you just stop trying to keep up. Do not let anyone grip you in their trip; you are meant to DO YOU outside of this energy. The Sacral is like a battery fuel that runs the world and pushes humanity to plug into it; wait, hold on! This sounds a lot like that movie reference again we all know and love. So, yup, they were right. It is time to unplug from the matrix, mainly if you are an Undefined Sacral. For those of you who are defined, then just only plug into something that satisfies you.

So for all you Undefined Sacrals out there, unplug from the Generator world, slow down, step back, unwind, relax. Maybe live in a place that costs you less, save some money, and instead of trying to keep up with the Joneses, just downscale a little so you can work less – what a concept. Let yourself live below your means, so if you need a break, you can take one. Don't worry; it is only when your energy is not taxed that you can categorically enjoy life. Someone press the button (meaning, let's blow this shit up) on the #hustle culture, and let's just trend #aligntoyourdesign. Wow, do you feel the shift? This is the new revolution, so do not be shocked. Just go get yourself some new sheets, a brand-new bed, and a pillow you love so you can sleep alone and enjoy your new throne – your bed! When you wake up again, you will be a majestic flowering goddess of the most high that all the world will seek out for insight and wisdom. Because the world needs your leadership now, it is time to set all the Sacral societal slaves FREE forever! So shall it be!

Here are some questions to answer if you have an Undefined (white) Sacral:

1. Am I burned out?
2. Am I overworking? Do I know when to stop? Do I know when enough is enough?
3. Am I using any type of addiction to deal with the discomfort of this energy?
4. Am I willing to sleep alone, try to step outside this force, and find my own energy field?

How the Not-Self might speak to those with an Undefined Sacral Center:

1. I can keep working; I just need a little lift or another shot of espresso.
2. I don't need a rest or sleep; let's just power through.
3. I have to hustle harder to keep up.
4. I have to grind more; no, I don't need boundaries.

Aligned and clear state for this Undefined Sacral: I am only working when I have energy. My energy aligns when I live my

Strategy and Inner Authority. I am confident that I do not need to fit in with the Generator world. I am safe and able to make a lot of money as myself, even if the world does not totally understand the power of working less yet. I am willing to do work in a new way. I am eager to live my life according to what is correct for me. I am ready to work less and charge more for my knowledge.

Aligned and clear state for a Defined Sacral: I am willing to only give my life force energy over to things that satisfy me. I am aware of my frustration, and I use this as a guide to wait to respond. I understand the response and will try not to push to initiate action. I am aware that not everyone is designed to keep up, and I will not compel others to do so.

Defined Sacral expressing itself in a distorted frequency or unhealthy way: Demanding that others keep up with you, judging those who need to rest, forcing the world to keep up, to work harder, to work longer hours in the world. Continuing with work which causes pain and frustration because it makes money, or you think you have to for some reason.

Meditation for the Undefined Sacral

Slow down, take a breath in, and let's all relax together. This is particularly important for you to make time and space to relax. You are allowed to sleep when you are tired, and you are allowed to be in the moment to trust your energy. You don't have to push; you don't have to do anything if you are tired. Feel the power in telling your friends or family no when you don't have the energy.

Your energy is your guide. If you are dragging or painfully exhausted, then just stop. Feel into the beauty of the slow-down revolution.

You are allowed to be calm, slow, know when enough is enough. You are special, don't compare yourself to anyone. You don't need to keep up. This doesn't mean that you are not as powerful. This doesn't mean anything about you. So let go of all your judgments around this. Free yourself from the helpless feeling of not having enough energy to keep up with those around you. Just let yourself be alone, have time to recoup, let yourself sleep more, relax more, be yourself. You are divine.

What pressures do you notice when you slow down? Do you feel the need to do something? Pay attention, allow, and just witness.

Congratulate yourself on the beginning journey of Deconditioning. They say this process takes a full seven years. But time is an illusion anyway, and there is nowhere you need to be, so relax, it's just time! You can't speed it up, so slow down and just surrender to it. Having everything you want that brings no satisfaction is 100% overrated and used solely as a marketing technique to keep you buying things. So, making things happen fast isn't always the titillating way to enjoy life. This process is about the juicy satisfaction of life, so don't rush it.

Knowing yourself is such a divine gift you are giving yourself, so honor the journey.

Chapter 15

What Does This Have to Do with Spiritual Awakening?

That is the real spiritual awakening when something emerges from within you that is deeper than who you thought you were. So, the person is still there, but one could almost say that something more powerful shines through the person.
Eckhart Tolle

As you discover who you are and align with your infinite genius, your Inner Authority and your Outer Authority represent your truth. This means that as you follow valiantly what is correct for you, live in the right timing, speak your wisdom to those who need it, Decondition from the Not-Self, sit back as a passenger, and witness life. You are you.

Some people refer to a completely aligned Inner/Outer authority as enlightenment. But please don't go around saying that Raquel now says, I am enlightened, or as some generation of kids say, I'm woke now. Please don't. Because being in your satisfaction flow isn't about showing your inner development to anyone else. It is about being it, living it, and feeling groovy from the inside out, for NO ONE else but you. This internal alignment, awe, peace is the greatest accomplishment to all life. So just revel in that. No, I didn't say I was enlightened either; just in case I get the Projection field here, I am far from mastering this. I am daily working on it and dedicated to the path, as I hope many of you are now as well.

As you awaken to your truth, it is not a contrived path. It is not something you can detail out because it is unique for each person. This is a very distinctively individual path of spiritual awakening.

However, it is also a practical path to live here on earth in your life, your career, your purpose in a way that feels the best to you. What a relief, just let go of all those things you thought you had to do and be your truth. WOW, what a novel idea!

With just a few tweaks, you can be flowering in your truth, living a life you love, allowing all to unfold slowly and perfectly. No one needs to work in a world or a life that feels horrible, or a life where you have to cut off your most unique aspects just to fit in.

This is your get-out-of-jail-free pass, the pass to stop doing what you hate, and a token to freedom to be yourself – the pass to be the beautiful Mutant you were born to be. Because we are all unique, we are all Mutants when we allow ourselves to De-condition from the homogenizing forces of society.

What I love so much about it is that you now get to understand how different your journey is, and instead of wishing you were someone else or had a different chart, you slowly fall in love with the unprecedented, singularity, sui generis that is YOU. You can become sovereign in yourself, and you never have to give your power away to another teacher, guru, religion, God, anyone, or anything else, ever again!

You are empowered TO BE YOURSELF.

This is the greatest gift I can give you, and in return you can give everyone in your inner circle and surrounding fractal.

As you go deeper into your Human Design contemplation, there are shadow aspects with each one of your Gates and Channels; once you contemplate your Design, you begin to awaken the SUPERPOWER hidden beneath the shadow. So yes, there is a lot more intel on the subject, so stay tuned for the next book in the series!

According to Ra Uru Hu, the plane of this teaching is intel on the mental plane. The spiritual plane is a little different, and yet merging the two leads to a path of spiritual alignment. So once your mind is a passenger and your vehicle can align with infinite intelligence, the spiritual awakening can begin its process. The biggest issue here, as with all spiritual teachings, is how do we control the mind?

Here we are learning how uniquely each person's mind operates and attacks them, allowing us to witness it more easily. Now you can quickly notice your shadows, discover who you are designed to be, then LET GO, SHUT UP, AND ENJOY THE RIDE!

O-BOOKS

SPIRITUALITY

O is a symbol of the world, of oneness and unity; this eye represents knowledge and insight. We publish titles on general spirituality and living a spiritual life. We aim to inform and help you on your own journey in this life.
If you have enjoyed this book, why not tell other readers by posting a review on your preferred book site?

Recent bestsellers from O-Books are:

Heart of Tantric Sex
Diana Richardson
Revealing Eastern secrets of deep love and intimacy to Western couples.
Paperback: 978-1-90381-637-0 ebook: 978-1-84694-637-0

Crystal Prescriptions
The A-Z guide to over 1,200 symptoms and their healing crystals
Judy Hall
The first in the popular series of eight books, this handy little guide is packed as tight as a pill-bottle with crystal remedies for ailments.
Paperback: 978-1-90504-740-6 ebook: 978-1-84694-629-5

Take Me To Truth
Undoing the Ego
Nouk Sanchez, Tomas Vieira
The best-selling step-by-step book on shedding the Ego, using the
teachings of *A Course In Miracles*.
Paperback: 978-1-84694-050-7 ebook: 978-1-84694-654-7

The 7 Myths about Love...Actually!
The Journey from your HEAD to the HEART of your SOUL
Mike George
Smashes all the myths about LOVE.
Paperback: 978-1-84694-288-4 ebook: 978-1-84694-682-0

The Holy Spirit's Interpretation of the New Testament
A Course in Understanding and Acceptance
Regina Dawn Akers
Following on from the strength of *A Course In Miracles*, NTI
teaches us how to experience the love and oneness of God.
Paperback: 978-1-84694-085-9 ebook: 978-1-78099-083-5

The Message of A Course In Miracles
A translation of the Text in plain language
Elizabeth A. Cronkhite
A translation of *A Course in Miracles* into plain, everyday
language for anyone seeking inner peace. The companion
volume, *Practicing A Course In Miracles*, offers practical lessons
and mentoring.
Paperback: 978-1-84694-319-5 ebook: 978-1-84694-642-4

Your Simple Path
Find Happiness in every step
Ian Tucker
A guide to helping us reconnect with what is really important in
our lives.
Paperback: 978-1-78279-349-6 ebook: 978-1-78279-348-9

365 Days of Wisdom
Daily Messages To Inspire You Through The Year
Dadi Janki
Daily messages which cool the mind, warm the heart and guide
you along your journey.
Paperback: 978-1-84694-863-3 ebook: 978-1-84694-864-0

Body of Wisdom
Women's Spiritual Power and How it Serves
Hilary Hart
Bringing together the dreams and experiences of women across
the world with today's most visionary spiritual teachers.
Paperback: 978-1-78099-696-7 ebook: 978-1-78099-695-0

Dying to Be Free
From Enforced Secrecy to Near Death to True Transformation
Hannah Robinson
After an unexpected accident and near-death experience, Hannah
Robinson found herself radically transforming her life, while a
remarkable new insight altered her relationship with her father, a
practising Catholic priest.
Paperback: 978-1-78535-254-6 ebook: 978-1-78535-255-3

The Ecology of the Soul
A Manual of Peace, Power and Personal Growth for Real People
in the Real World
Aidan Walker
Balance your own inner Ecology of the Soul to regain your
natural state of peace, power and wellbeing.
Paperback: 978-1-78279-850-7 ebook: 978-1-78279-849-1

Not I, Not other than I
The Life and Teachings of Russel Williams
Steve Taylor, Russel Williams
The miraculous life and inspiring teachings of one of the World's
greatest living Sages.
Paperback: 978-1-78279-729-6 ebook: 978-1-78279-728-9

On the Other Side of Love
A woman's unconventional journey towards wisdom
Muriel Maufroy
When life has lost all meaning, what do you do?
Paperback: 978-1-78535-281-2 ebook: 978-1-78535-282-9

Practicing A Course In Miracles
A translation of the Workbook in plain language, with
mentor's notes
Elizabeth A. Cronkhite
The practical second and third volumes of The Plain-Language
A Course In Miracles.
Paperback: 978-1-84694-403-1 ebook: 978-1-78099-072-9

Quantum Bliss
The Quantum Mechanics of Happiness, Abundance, and Health
George S. Mentz
Quantum Bliss is the breakthrough summary of success and spirituality secrets that customers have been waiting for.
Paperback: 978-1-78535-203-4 ebook: 978-1-78535-204-1

The Upside Down Mountain
Mags MacKean
A must-read for anyone weary of chasing success and happiness – one woman's inspirational journey swapping the uphill slog for the downhill slope.
Paperback: 978-1-78535-171-6 ebook: 978-1-78535-172-3

Your Personal Tuning Fork
The Endocrine System
Deborah Bates
Discover your body's health secret, the endocrine system, and 'twang' your way to sustainable health!
Paperback: 978-1-84694-503-8 ebook: 978-1-78099-697-4

Readers of ebooks can buy or view any of these bestsellers by clicking on the live link in the title. Most titles are published in paperback and as an ebook. Paperbacks are available in traditional bookshops. Both print and ebook formats are available online.
Find more titles and sign up to our readers' newsletter at http://www.johnhuntpublishing.com/mind-body-spirit
Follow us on Facebook at https://www.facebook.com/OBooks/ and Twitter at https://twitter.com/obooks